PEACE AND CONFLICT SERIES
Ron Milam, General Editor

ALSO IN THIS SERIES:
Crooked Bamboo: A Memoir from Inside the Diem Regime
by Nguyen Thai; edited by Justin Simundson

Girls Don't! A Woman's War in Vietnam
by Inette Miller

Rain in Our Hearts: Alpha Company in the Vietnam War
by James Allen Logue and Gary D. Ford

Conscientious Objectors at War

The Vietnam War's Forgotten Medics

GARY KULIK

TEXAS TECH UNIVERSITY PRESS

Copyright © 2025 by Gary Kulik

All rights reserved. No portion of this book may be reproduced in any form or by any means, including electronic storage and retrieval systems, except by explicit prior written permission of the publisher. Brief passages excerpted for review and critical purposes are excepted.

This book is typeset in EB Garamond. The paper used in this book meets the minimum requirements of ANSI/NISO Z39.48-1992 (R1997). ∞

Designed by Hannah Gaskamp
Cover design by Hannah Gaskamp
Cover photograph by Bettmann via Getty Images

Library of Congress Cataloging-in-Publication Data

Names: Kulik, Gary author / Title: Conscientious Objectors at War: The Forgotten Medics of the Vietnam War / Gary Kulik. Other titles: Forgotten medics of the Vietnam War Description: Lubbock, Texas: Texas Tech University Press, 2025. | Series: Peace and Conflict | Includes bibliographical references and index. | Summary: "Stories of conscientious objector medics during the Vietnam War with a background context of pacifist churches in America"—Provided by publisher.
Identifiers: LCCN 2024060142 (print) | LCCN 2024060143 (ebook) | ISBN 978-1-68283-260-8 paperback | ISBN 978-1-68283-261-5 ebook
Subjects: LCSH: Vietnam War, 1961–1975—Conscientious objectors—United States | Vietnam War, 1961–1975—Medical care—United States | United States. Army—Medical personnel
Classification: LCC DS559.8.C63 K85 2025 (print) | LCC DS559.8.C63 (ebook) | DDC 959.704/37—/eng/20250306
LC record available at https://lccn.loc.gov/2024060142
LC ebook record available at https://lccn.loc.gov/2024060143

Texas Tech University Press
Box 41037
Lubbock, Texas 79409-1037 USA
800.832.4042
ttup@ttu.edu
www.ttupress.org

To My Fellow Conscientious Objector Medics
Who Served in Vietnam

Contents

PREFACE		ix
ACKNOWLEDGMENTS		xi
	Introduction	3
CHAPTER 1:	Historical Background to Noncombatant Service	13
CHAPTER 2:	A California Pantheist	33
CHAPTER 3:	A Roman Catholic from New Jersey	47
CHAPTER 4:	Five Adventists from the Mid-Atlantic	57
CHAPTER 5:	A Death in Khe Sanh	69
CHAPTER 6:	Three Memoirs	81
CHAPTER 7:	Stories of Courage and Loss	97
CHAPTER 8:	A Poet Returns from War	115
	Epilogue	125
NOTES		129
SELECTED BIBLIOGRAPHY		157
INDEX		163

Preface

On one level this is a conventional scholarly book composed of oral history, interviews, and the close reading of secondary sources, memoirs, and a small number of poems. It is focused on those who served as conscientious objector medics (CO medics) in Vietnam, including two who acted as conscientious objectors who had not been so designated. This book excludes those CO medics who served elsewhere, all those who sought alternative service, and all those who filed as conscientious objectors seeking discharge after enlisting. Within its focus, the book makes no claims to be representative of all those who served as CO medics in Vietnam. This is then a grouping of individual stories of men who made fraught and morally distinctive decisions in the face of an unpopular war—to serve as unarmed medics. May it lead to more such books.

At another level, this is an unconventional and deeply personal book. Some may find it intrusively personal, for this is my story too. I found that I simply could not tell these stories from an Olympian height. So readers will notice my own comments interspersed, sometimes affirming a common experience, sometimes not, and occasionally offering a differing moral valence. Choosing to serve as a CO medic in Vietnam was the most significant moral decision of my life and I have not been able, in writing this book, to put that behind me. So be it.

We are now more than fifty years away from the time that conscientious objection was widely understood. An introductory note may be helpful to readers. During the Vietnam War, men opposed to all wars and to all killing applied to their draft boards as conscientious objectors. The vast majority sought alternative service, in hospitals and other social service agencies approved by their draft boards. A much smaller number agreed to serve in uniform as unarmed medics. An even smaller number of absolutists for whom no form of service was morally acceptable paid the heavy price of prison.

For those brought up in the traditional peace churches, for whom the Sixth Commandment was either literal truth or felt practice—Quakers, Brethren, Mennonites—the path to conscientious objection was clear and straightforward. The Seventh-day Adventist Church came to define its draft-eligible young men, as a marker of its civic patriotism and as a distancing from the older peace churches, as "conscientious cooperators" willing to serve as medics. Those raised as Catholics, Methodists, Episcopalians, and in other mainstream churches adhering to "just war" beliefs found their own way to forms of pacifism largely rooted in Christian ethics and belief. A smaller number of COs embraced Gandhian, Buddhist, or Bahá'í beliefs. With the Supreme Court's decision in *United States v. Seeger* (1965), increasing numbers of COs based their claims on secular and humanitarian argument though at times with an implicit acknowledgement of Christian teaching. Selective conscientious objection—opposition to the war in Vietnam alone—was never legal.

Conscientious objection, for those who served in the Vietnam War, was not binary. Some chose to carry weapons, some to use them. For those who have never been to war, this may seem discrediting. It's better to be seen as just another of the moral complexities, the "greyness" I write about in the introduction, faced by those who sought to honor both duty and conscience.

Acknowledgments

My grateful thanks to those who served as CO medics in Vietnam and to family members of COs who died in Vietnam who responded to my entreaties: Karen and Robert Abrahamson, Donita Brownlee, Sandy Cole, the Rev. Mike Dingman, Ron Donahey, the Rev. William Hall, Tom Hirst, Basil Paquet, David Rogers, Mike Rogers, Doug Settle, Karen and the late Terry Sewell, Larry Sluiter, the Rev. Ray Stubbe, Dan Sullivan, and Ray Wenger.

Thanks to the staff at the Vietnam Center and Sam Johnson Vietnam Archive, Texas Tech University, Stephen Maxner, Amy K. Mondt, Kelly Crager, and Laura Calkins; to the staff of the Seventh-day Adventist Church Archive, Silver Spring, Maryland, and a special thanks to Bill Knott, then editor of *Adventist World*, and to Dr. Benjamin Butler; and to Duane B. Miller and the staff of the US Army Heritage and Education Center, Carlisle, Pennsylvania.

I offered portions of the introduction at the Texas Tech University, Vietnam Center conference "A Medical History of the Vietnam War" in San Antonio, Texas, in March 2016. My thanks to Stephen Maxner and the conference organizers. I spoke from the introduction again at St. Michael's College, Colchester, Vermont, in February 2018, as the Norbert A. Kuntz Memorial Lecturer, sponsored by the Edmundite Center for Faith and Culture and the History Department, with special thanks to Fr. David J. Theroux, Fr. Marcel Rainville, Jennifer J. Purcell, Rowena Xiaoqing He, and then President John J. Neuhauser.

I am grateful for the encouragement of Peter Zinoman, Randall Miller, and Marshall Poe. Marshall, the founder of the podcast *New Books Network*, introduced me to Krzysztof Odyniec, who runs the affiliated podcast *Almost*

Good Catholics and who interviewed me in March 2023: "Gary Kulik: Conscientious Objector Who Served in Vietnam."

Grateful thanks to Patrick Malone, Jon Butler, John W. Chambers II, and Gilbert Valentine who read and commented on portions of the typescript and recommended further reading. Professor Valentine connected me to Kevin Burton at the Center for Adventist Research, Andrews University, who kindly shared with me his forthcoming article.

I had the pleasure to meet with fellow CO medic Bill Clamurro, and to support the compelling book that he and James Kearney would publish, *Duty to Serve, Duty to Conscience: The Story of Two Conscientious Objector Combat Medics during the Vietnam War*.

Many thanks to Travis Snyder, editor in chief; the staff, especially Joanna Conrad, Christie Perlmutter, Eytan Pol, Hannah Gaskamp, and John Brock; and the anonymous readers of Texas Tech University Press for their commitment and support. I am gratefully in their debt. Special thanks also to Heidi Zimmerman, Vietnam Veterans Memorial Fund, and Liz Rathbun, *ARMY* magazine, for their help on photo research. And sincere thanks to Michelle Guiliano for preparing the index.

Words cannot fully express my love and gratitude to Barbara Melosh, wife, author, pastor. Her support transcended the occasional editorial comments and the software fixes, as valuable as they were. I could not have written this book without her.

Conscientious Objectors at War

Introduction

During the war in Vietnam, as many as 15,000 young men served as conscientious objectors (COs) in the US Army. I was one. The term conscientious objector doesn't really seem to fit those of us who wore the uniform of our country and went to war as I did. To be a conscientious objector suggests something absolute, men refusing induction, risking jail or worse, or, at the very least, men refusing to don a uniform and seeking to serve their country in more pacific ways.[1]

The right of conscientious objection was first acknowledged by the federal government of the United States during the Civil War. That right, however, applied only to members of traditional peace churches—Quakers, Brethren, Mennonites—whose understanding of the Sixth Commandment (Thou Shalt Not Kill) was literal and absolute. The 1940 draft law opened an opportunity for all those who "by religious training and belief [are] conscientiously opposed to war in any form," and so Catholics, Episcopalians, Lutherans, Methodists, and others could be COs, not because their churches embraced pacifism but because they did as individuals and because they could root their belief in their understanding of their faith. The law has since evolved to embrace those whose objections to killing and to service are ethical rather than religious.[2]

The law at the time offered two paths to conscientious objection, and that decision rested in the hands of local draft boards. One path, for those whose religious beliefs not only proscribed killing but also proscribed service in the military, led to alternative duties, such as civilian hospital work or its moral equivalents. The second path led to service in the military as a noncombatant, defined in the early years of World War II as service as an Army medic. Those who chose service as noncombatant army medics in the Vietnam era were a tiny minority—15,000 or so compared to 171,700 men who sought alternative service in the years from 1960 to 1973.³

The term noncombatant doesn't get it quite right. The vast majority of medics were attached to infantry divisions. They may not have carried weapons, but many knew combat. Every infantry platoon—every thirty men—needs a medic, with many more medics in reserve. The army trained 210,404 medics in the years 1963–1972—a number exceeded only by infantry riflemen. A rough estimate from a former commander of the US Army Medical Training Center is that 6 to 8 percent of Army medics were COs—thus the estimated number of 15,000. Not all, however, served in Vietnam. There is no official accounting of how many CO medics served in Vietnam, and I've found no way to estimate the numbers. My memory is that most of my medical training class, graduating in the fall of 1969, went directly to Vietnam, the others to Germany.⁴

I went to Washington in a cushy assignment arranged by the then Speaker of the House, John McCormack. My family was well connected politically. However, when the May 1970 levy for Vietnam reached me, the efforts of my command, endorsed at the highest levels at Walter Reed Medical Center to retain me in Washington, were overruled by Pentagon bureaucrats. The need for medics in Vietnam remained overwhelming. Shamed by my use of political influence to avoid Vietnam service, I accepted my orders.

The story of CO medics in Vietnam is a compelling story of conscience, honor—halting honor in my case—and, on some occasions, of extraordinary heroism. Two COs were awarded the Medal of Honor, posthumously. Yet it is a story largely unknown. There is no history of CO medics in Vietnam, indeed no history of those who chose alternative service. At one level this is surprising, given the great volume of books on Vietnam-era dissent, on draft resistance, on draft avoidance, on desertion, on migration to Canada, and on the antiwar movement among GIs.⁵

Yet maybe it isn't so surprising. Many of those books on war resistance were written in the red heat of the moment and that moment lingers. War resisters were often seen as the true heroes of the war. In a black and white world, men who willingly served don't easily fit. We occupy a grey zone. Our moral dissent was not as absolute as for those who chose prison or alternative service. We were not war resisters. We went to war, complicit, as some would say, in the larger evils of that war, or, as the more recent dispensations would have it, as naïve victims.

I lived in that grey zone and, as my writings on the war evidence, I continue to inhabit it. Like many young men and women on the left in those years, I was opposed to the war. I thought it morally wrong. We were supporting a corrupt government, I was sure then, and I came to embrace the widely-held antiwar sentiment that the Viet Cong were a largely independent force reflecting core beliefs of the Vietnamese people, that Hồ Chí Minh and his followers were fighting principally for national independence, that the North was reluctantly drawn into war because of the United States's refusal to allow national elections in 1956, and should the North prevail, an outcome some on the far left supported, that they would be humane victors. We now know—or should know—how naïve and wrong those beliefs were. But that's what I felt then.[6]

There was little in my earliest religious training that led to this, but I found my way, with the help of friends, to the writings of Dorothy Day, Thomas Merton, Daniel Berrigan. My church was capacious enough to offer the intellectual and theological resources I needed. When I took up my studies at St. Michael's College, twelve credits of theology and another twelve of neo-Thomist philosophy were required of all students. I added another six credits of philosophy. It was that training that allowed me to address the critical question that I knew someone on the draft board would ask: Would I have served in World War II? Deep in my heart, I knew that the answer was yes. But the question was hypothetical and anachronistic. How could I be morally sure of what I would have done four years before my birth? And so I came to believe I could not answer the question with moral certainty, an argument that any Thomist (never affirm, rarely deny, always distinguish) would have understood. I could not then and cannot now claim a principled pacifism. Grey indeed.[7]

I chose to serve, not fully realizing that Vietnam was my probable destination, but even if I had been more prescient, I doubt that I would have chosen differently. I had grown up in a family closely tied to the military. My father was a World War II veteran and remained active as an officer in the Air Force Reserve. His two brothers were service academy graduates (West Point and Annapolis) still on active duty. Our tours in Vietnam would overlap. I had a deep respect and love for all of them. I never felt the anger and contempt some of my peers directed then at the military. Moreover, I had no desire to spend two years emptying bedpans, and with a certain hard pragmatism, I doubted I could convince a Springfield, Massachusetts, draft board, likely comprising several Catholic members, that my religious beliefs precluded uniformed service.

There were of course other choices. For reasons both moral and political, I could not embrace them. I was unwilling to serve as an officer in a war I opposed, unwilling to use influence to join the National Guard (whose true purpose in those years was to eliminate the risks of war for those with the right connections), and, caught up in that 1960s quest for moral authenticity, unwilling to fake an exempting medical condition, though I soon learned how rare was my choice. I wasn't going to Canada or to jail, so I raised my right hand that June day, though not before writing on my induction form that I knew the difference between legal and illegal orders and that I intended to disobey all illegal orders. The induction sergeant that day, showing what could only have been my form to another staffer, said: "We'll let the UCMJ [the Uniform Code of Military Justice] deal with him." But I had said nothing that contradicted the UCMJ. Soldiers have a duty not to follow illegal orders, though that was a duty not widely taught at the time.

In a few days, I was on my way to Fort Sam Houston, to a surviving portion of the Long Barracks, built between 1885 and 1892—the home of CO basic training since 1954. I had no knowledge then that I was one of many thousands—a long green line of COs—about to begin a truncated six-week version (everything but the rifle range) of army basic training. But had I had that knowledge then, I doubt that I would have been appreciative. There was for me something oppressive about these nineteenth-century barracks, made worse by the heat of a Texas summer and by the murals decorating the barracks walls, painted no doubt by former trainees, depicting the courage and honor of combat medics in a style that can best be called military kitsch, a form of art intended to lift morale while whitewashing the true costs of courage and honor.[8]

Yet, with one exception—a borderline sadist of a buck sergeant—I have only positive memories of the enlisted training staff. My senior drill sergeants—the men with the Smokey Bear hats—were tough but fair. I came to respect them and I continue to honor them by making sure that my shoes are always properly shined.

My basic training class was divided roughly in half. One platoon was made up of an eclectic mix of Catholics and mainline Protestants, many of whom had come to their beliefs against the grain of their churches' just-war theologies, along with Quakers and Brethren, the sons of traditional peace churches. As a group they were well educated, articulate. Opposed to the war in Vietnam, they had staked out positions that were moral rather than narrowly political. I had little opportunity to interact with them. A small group of us similar in makeup were consigned to a platoon dominated by Seventh-day Adventists (SDA). The SDAs were followers of Ellen White, the nineteenth-century American co-founder of a church based on Biblical literalism, a faith-based diet free of meat and alcohol (yes, there were vegetarian options in the mess hall), and a belief in the imminent return of Jesus Christ. In my memory, they tended to be younger and apolitical, with higher numbers of African Americans and high school–only graduates than the non-SDAs. There was one aspect of their faith that rankled. Their Sabbath was Saturday, a half-day training day with make-work filling the afternoon for the rest of us, while they were excused from duty. They covered for us on Sundays, of course, a day when few cadres were in evidence and work duties were light. By the end of training, I had made friends with one SDA, a college graduate from New York City, and in doing research recently at the SDA global headquarters, I have come to a deeper and more positive view of this distinctively American religion and its adherents.[9]

Once we moved across post to begin medical training, our status as COs could effectively disappear. No one shouldered arms in medical training, so if we chose to say nothing no one would know. I was the only CO in my platoon. My memory is that I spoke about my CO status selectively, only with men I thought would understand. There was a moment in our medical training when one of our numbers noticed a nearby basic training exercise involving the latest class of COs. He seemed convinced that drill sergeants were especially harsh in their treatment of COs. That wasn't my experience. I chose, however, to say nothing. If my fellow medical trainee wanted to believe that COs were brutalized in basic training, so be it.

COs could remain anonymous only so long. Once assigned to a company in Vietnam, all COs were faced with an existential decision, a true test of what had started simply as words on paper and words spoken to a draft board. Mine happened when the company clerk from Headquarters & Alpha Company, 4th Medical Battalion, drove out to the 4th Infantry Division training area, where men new in-country learned what they would likely face, with an M16 for me. I said no. "What are you going to do, kill them with your bare hands?" a fellow medic asked. However, I accompanied my fellow newbies to the rifle range and to a class on the new protocols for field-stripping the rifle. I came away believing that I knew enough to load, aim, and fire an M16. In extremis, I have no doubt I would have armed myself. I was never faced with the need.

There is no way of knowing how many COs carried weapons. Some did, at least on occasion. A fellow CO in my company told me he accepted a .45 pistol offered to him by a platoon sergeant while in a night ambush position. Tom Hirst was an SDA medic assigned to the 1st Cavalry Division in early 1970. On his way to join a field unit, he was offered a .45 and chose an M16 instead, a "patient protector," he wrote, in a website post. Hirst saw combat—his company was sent into Cambodia in the spring of 1970.[10]

And so after refusing that rifle, I found myself in June 1970 in my company's clearing platoon, assigned to the aid station at Camp Radcliff, on the outskirts of An Khê, Bình Định Province. In an area once rife with main force Viet Cong and North Vietnamese Army units, Bình Định Province was now relatively quiet. Viet Cong units suffered heavy losses during the Tet Offensive in 1968. I was the beneficiary of that. The 4th Infantry had recently relocated from Pleiku to An Khê in preparation for returning to Fort Carson in the fall—though I knew none of that at the time.

I benefited in other ways as well. I was a college graduate with a year of graduate school. I presume that I had scored well on the army's intelligence tests. And so I was assigned to the battalion's headquarters company, a safer place than the battalion's other companies located on fire bases, and far safer than infantry line companies. We provided medics for day and a half perimeter patrol, and I was so assigned. I treated one wounded soldier. When the 4th went home, I was reassigned to a helicopter medevac (dustoff) battalion. Asked if I could type, I said yes, but I wanted the opportunity to fly, to serve as a dustoff medic—a quest stymied by less than perfect vision. And so I served out my time in another headquarters company, as clerk to the battalion adjutant, leaving Vietnam two months early—the result of an early-out to study French at New York University in preparation for my doctoral exams. I had an easy war.

Needless to say, my CO medic story cannot stand as representative of that of all CO medics. The more I think about the men I trained with, served with, and now read about, what resonates is how different we were and how different were our experiences—young and enthusiastic SDAs, some of whom had been members of church-sponsored Medical Cadet Corps in high school, almost all of whom in the years of the war sought to enter the Whitecoat program, volunteering for medical experimentation at Fort Detrick, Maryland, ensuring that they would never serve in Vietnam—a complicated and poorly understood story; a former Catholic seminarian whose calm and quiet faith drew me to him in basic training who believed that his witness required him to serve in Vietnam, this at a time when I was not prepared to drink from that cup; a Catholic from New Jersey who served in combat with the 1st Infantry Division and who returned his medals on the Capitol grounds in the veterans' antiwar protest in the spring of 1971. In a recent interview, he told me he could not receive communion for years, so deep were his feelings of guilt and complicity. Then a young man from California who told his draft board that he was a pantheist—his draft board bought it—and who in Vietnam incongruously formed a friendship with a fellow soldier guilty of war crimes. Then there was a Jew from Detroit, the same medic who told me he took a weapon in a night ambush position, who chose to identify himself on the piss tubes that marked our weekly adherence to the army's malaria protocol not by his name or serial number, but with an aggressive in-your-face humor—Jew, he wrote. But he wasn't a Jew, he told me in a recent phone call. He claimed to be Jewish solely to qualify for extended leave during the High Holidays. On a lighter note, I met a preventive medicine specialist, an inspector of piss tubes and latrines, who professed the Baháʼí faith and who looked forward to returning home to his wife who always chose to lie next to him should he nap (it's odd what we remember from that time). Then there was an Episcopalian, a fourth-generation Californian, who once sent a bottle of wine back at a meal we shared with two stewardesses on R&R in Hong Kong. Those of us who served in Vietnam as COs were neither easily predictable as types nor models of moral consistency. Some of us sought to avoid Vietnam service. Some of us took up weapons.

We were a strange and complicated lot. Most of us did our jobs. Few of us were heroes. Not all of us came home. Thomas W. Bennett, a CO medic in Bravo Company, 1st Battalion, 14th Infantry, 4th Infantry Division, was awarded the Medal of Honor, posthumously, for his repeated efforts to tend to wounded soldiers in Pleiku Province, 11 February 1969. There is a building named for him at West Virginia University. He was a Southern Baptist.[11]

Roger Clayton Brathwaite, born in the West Indies, a member of a Pentecostal church, served as a CO medic in Delta Company, 1st Battalion, 327th Infantry, 101st Airborne Division. He died from "multiple fragmentation wounds" 16 July 1969. A chaplain and a veteran medic had persuaded him to carry an M16. Dave Shade, who served with him but knew him only as the Black medic who had once saved his life, honored him in a long and emotional website post. Michael Moreno, who also served with him, wrote: "Your death was not in vain. You gave something, to the rest of us, something, that can never be repaid."[12]

Gary Lee Abrahamson, born in Iowa in 1951, raised in the Adventist faith, was one of the last CO medics to die. Serving with the 198th Light Infantry Brigade, Abrahamson was shot in the chest in an NDP (night defensive position) near Mỹ Đồng, 20 Sept 1970. The first medevac flight crashed. The second was too late to save him.[13]

INTRODUCTION

In reflecting, some fifty years later, on my own reluctant but conscience-driven service, as well as on the service of my fellow COs, I remain deeply divided, a long-term resident of that grey zone. I've written elsewhere that the United States had every right and every duty to assist the South Vietnamese from a communist takeover, but we had no business taking over the war—sending ground troops into Vietnam. Those of us who served were betrayed by politicians and generals. And yet I resist any notion that we—my fellow CO medics—were victims. We made hard moral choices—choosing to do justice in the face of a greater injustice. Those choices were ours, defining us then, defining us now.[14]

CHAPTER 1

Historical Background to Noncombatant Service

There is no single volume history of conscientious objection or pacifism in America. The published work available focuses on specific periods or on specific wars. Most such work slights the history of noncombatant service, choosing instead to emphasize alternative service and the small number of "absolutists" who served time in prisons rather than perform alternative service or enlist as noncombatants. What follows below is an attempt to provide the necessary historical background to noncombatant service in order to better understand the choices and the experiences of the many men who served as unarmed medics in the Vietnam War.[1]

Pacifism came to the American colonies from the radical edges of Protestantism. Quakers, members of the Society of Friends founded in England in the mid-seventeenth century, were the first to bring the testimony of peace to American shores. Theirs was a belief rooted in the "Inner Light." For Quakers, according to a leading historian of American pacifism, "peace came to mean following the way of love that begins in the hearts of individuals and through them leavens society until all men are won."[2]

In moments of crisis, when the colonies faced the backwash of European wars or when Native tribes resisted the encroaching frontiers of settlement, Quakers insisted that their "scrupulous" opposition to war forbade them from both serving in the militia and paying to support a common defense, though some did pay. Even Pennsylvania, the colony founded by Quakers, disagreed. Quakers who refused wartime support suffered "distraint of property," the confiscation of wagons and teams, of blankets and food. Joseph Townsend, a Quaker whose home was near the Battle of Brandywine, resisted a colonial officer's demand that he take down fencing so that his troops could pass. The fence came down. As a faithful Quaker, Townsend was not allowed to seek monetary recompense at the cost of disownment.[3]

A second stream of pacifism emerged earlier from the Anabaptist tradition during the years of Reformation in Europe. The legatees of that tradition—Moravians, Mennonites, and smaller German sects—settled in Southern and mid-Atlantic colonies in the eighteenth century. They differed from the Quakers. Their pacifism was rooted exclusively in scripture, not in the "Inner Light" of conscience. They weren't interested in political power. Their pacifism, or non-resistance, was more flexible than the Quakers'. They were not opposed to hiring a substitute for militia service, or to contributing to the common defense by offering wagons and teams of horses for use by the militia.[4]

On the eve of the American Revolution, the long struggle waged by the colonies' peace churches had largely been won. Most of the colonies accommodated the claims of conscience asserted by Quakers, Mennonites, and smaller German sects. Virginia, North Carolina, and, for a time, Rhode Island offered blanket exemptions. New York, New Jersey, and Pennsylvania offered exemptions that required those unwilling to serve to either pay a fine or hire a substitute. The failure to do so would result in the confiscation of property or imprisonment for those without property.[5]

The claims of conscience were so well understood by 1787 that James Madison once proposed protecting those "religiously scrupulous of bearing arms" as a part of the Second Amendment of the Bill of Rights. Madison's words did not survive debate that Philadelphia summer, in part because the newly forming states had their own history of protecting such scruples.[6]

The Civil War would pose the first national test to the claims of conscience. When it became clear that volunteers to serve the Union were insufficient to the needs of the North, Congress passed the Federal Enrollment

Act of 3 March 1863. The Act authorized the drafting of men between the ages of 20 and 45 while allowing the hiring of substitutes or the payment of a commutation of $300, which was a considerable sum. The Act provoked violent dissent in the North, leading to draft riots in multiple cities and especially in New York where recent Irish immigrants and others, in fear for their jobs and in the grip of a vile racism, visited violence and murder upon African Americans.[7]

The Act contained no provision for conscientious objection. The Friends were quick to object. A delegation of Baltimore Friends called on William Stanton, Secretary of War. Stanton respected the Friends' beliefs and proposed that Friends exempted from the draft could apply their $300 fee not to support the war but to assist recently freed slaves, the monies to be managed by the Friends themselves.[8]

A revised conscription bill of 24 February 1864 contained a version of Stanton's proposal while offering, for the first time, a form of noncombatant military service. The act stipulated that those who are "conscientiously opposed to the bearing of arms and who are prohibited from doing so ... by the articles of faith and practice" of their denominations may be drafted into the military as "non-combatants," assigned "to duty in the hospitals or to the care of freedmen." The bill provided a second path for religious objectors. The $300 commutation fee, open under the new law only to religious objectors, could be "applied to the benefit of the sick and wounded soldiers." The Civil War laws in the North thus provided the template—noncombatant service linked to medical care—that would become the exclusive form of noncombatant service from World War II to the Vietnam War. But such service was then only available to the members of churches theologically committed to pacifism.[9]

These new concessions to conscience did not move Quaker true believers who insisted that only unconditional exemption could satisfy their scruples: no commutation, no substitutes, no noncombatant service. There is no better example than Cyrus Pringle. A recent convert to Quakerism from Vermont, with the zeal of the newly converted, Pringle was drafted in July 1863. He would later become a distinguished botanist—the Pringle Herbarium at the University of Vermont is named for him. His Civil War diary, published in 1913 and twice reprinted, is a singular account of a fierce Quaker conscience in the years of war.[10]

Refusing to pay commutation, despite the advice of acquaintances, Pringle wrote of his four-month travails as he journeyed from Rutland to Boston to Culpepper, Virginia. Initially treated with "sympathy," he was excused from duty and drill. But when he refused to perform "Fatigue Duty" in Boston, he and another Friend were remanded to the guardhouse. He would be treated even more harshly in Virginia, staked out on the ground for two hours, threatened with courts-martial and even death for refusing to clean his rifle. On two occasions, military commanders offered Pringle the option of noncombatant hospital service. Elder Friends urged him to do so. He couldn't: "Oh the cruelest blow of all comes from our friends" was his response to the first offer. His refusal of the second offer, however, acknowledged a more nuanced emotion: "We seem to be liable … to be exposed to the charge of overzeal and fanaticism even among our own brethren."[11]

In the fall of 1863, Friends, with influence in Washington, had come to Pringle's aid. Ordered to Washington, Pringle met with a Colonel Townsend, the Adjutant General. He was told that both President Lincoln and Stanton would grant him "full release," but it was not yet expedient. He would have to serve for a time at a hospital in New York City. He consented to this third hospital offer because he believed that the caregivers were all civilian nurses and that he would not be taking the place of a soldier who could be ordered to war. He would find out otherwise, but by then his ill health had confined him to bed. Still sick, he learned of Lincoln's offer of "parole," allowing him to return home in early November 1863. Lincoln's sense of mercy was clear. We may have a harder time judging Pringle—a high-minded idealist or an uncompromising zealot?[12]

Pringle was an exception. Other young Friends, motivated in part by opposition to slavery, joined the Union Army. One study suggested that one-fifth to one-quarter of Indiana Friends from eight counties served in uniform. Others, such as their Mennonite brethren, were willing to pay commutation, especially after the 1864 act allowed the money to be used for the benefit of the sick and wounded.[13]

There were other smaller sects and communities that embraced pacifism—the Rogerenes of Connecticut, the Shakers, the communitarians at Amana in Iowa, those at Hopedale in Massachusetts—but none would be more important to the future of noncombatant service than the Seventh-day Adventists. The Adventists, inspired by the prophecies of Ellen Gould White, a native of Maine, were the most successful remnant of the broader Adventist movement inspired by William Miller and his followers who believed that Jesus would return to earth by 1844. Ellen White was successful in redefining the Millerite prophecy after what came to be known as "The Great Disappointment." White, along with her husband James, founded a church imbued with the emotional fervor of the Second Great Awakening, a church committed to a Saturday Sabbath and a firm belief in the imminent return of Jesus: "the great day of God," she wrote, "is right upon us."[14]

The Whites and their followers adhered to an ambitious reform agenda. They embraced dietary reform—no meat, no tobacco, no alcohol. Residing mostly in the North, they were opposed to slavery. William Lloyd Garrison had influenced some of their number. They understood that the Sixth Commandment forbade killing. But in the midst of Civil War they were a new and small church, not formally established until 1863, with fewer than 4,000 members. They needed to make their case to the civil authorities, but it appears that their leadership did not have a clear or consistent pacifist position on the Civil War.[15]

The revised conscription act of February 1864 which opened noncombatant service to the members of pacifist churches offered Adventist leaders the opportunity to clarify their theology. The Adventists made the case that they were a pacifist church, ignoring internal dissent, with a flurry of successful petitions to the governors of Michigan, Wisconsin, Illinois, Pennsylvania, and to the federal Provost Marshall, Brigadier General James Fry, in August 1864. We have accounts of two Adventist draftees who chose to pay commutation and another account suggesting that "most [Adventist] draftees" entered the army and opted for "hospital and freedmen work"—the first Adventist noncombatants but not the last. Yet we also have evidence that young Adventists took up arms and joined the Union Army. They too were the first to do so, but also not the last.[16]

CHAPTER I

World War I

When President Woodrow Wilson made the decision to ask Congress to declare war against Germany in April 1917, he did so knowing that a new national draft would be necessary. There was opposition to both the war and the draft from a disparate assembly of socialists, feminists, Midwestern progressives, and Southern farmers, joined by the odd industrialist such as Andrew Carnegie and Henry Ford. Their dissent was overwhelmed by a Congress that voted for war 373–50 in the House, and 82–6 in the Senate. The vote for conscription was even more decisive—only 32 members of Congress voted no.[17]

The Selective Service Act of May 1917, which was not random conscription but targeted selection, differed from the Civil War draft in the North. This time there would be no possibility of hiring substitutes or of paying commutation, provisions long seen as favoring the wealthy. But these were also measures that were embraced by many conscientious objectors during the Civil War. Now their choices had narrowed, and the consequences for Mennonites and the smaller German sects would prove dire.[18]

The Wilson administration had no better initial solution than to offer a variant of the language of the Civil War draft. Members of "any well-recognized religious sect . . . whose principles forbid its members to participate in war in any form" would not have to shoulder arms, but they would have to serve as noncombatants. But the term was not defined and it would remain undefined for months.[19]

There was another important difference from the time of the Civil War. The ranks of the peace churches had increased. Quakers and Mennonites had been joined by Adventists and also by a bewildering array of little-known sects— Russellites (later known as Jehovah's Witnesses), along with Molokans from Russia, who emigrated to avoid military service, as did the Hutterites, in addition to Christadelphians, members of the Church of God and the Saints of Christ, and the Israelite House of David, among others. Not every draft board, in the absence of clear national guidance, was equipped to understand such varied claims.[20]

And for the first time, men of conscience from mainstream churches asserted claims of pacifism grounded in personal religious belief. Then, there were the political objectors, socialists, anarchists, and others. By one estimate, three-quarters of objectors came from peace churches, 15 percent from mainstream churches; 10 percent were political objectors.[21]

When training camps first opened in mid-September 1917, the War Department appeared to have no plan for what would happen to conscientious objectors interspersed with men ready to train for battle. It was, according to David M. Kennedy, the leading historian of the war's impact on America, "the most callous feature of government policy." Some objectors faced the hostility of peers as well as officers and sergeants. One Hutterite at Camp Funston in late September 1917 wrote of men beaten, others plunged in water as if to drown them—"the soldiers had rifles, revolvers, and sticks and used them in godless ways."[22]

Camp Funston's commander, Maj. Gen. Leonard Woods, gave voice to a belief that objectors were "enemies of the Republic, fakers, and active agents of the enemy." Former president Theodore Roosevelt had incited such beliefs in several addresses in 1917, claiming the conscientious objector's unwillingness to kill only "curtained his cowardice," and that the loudest among them "are paid or unpaid agents of the German government," while others were the "white handed or sissy type" who represented only decadence. Objectors were thus shirkers, cowards, sissies, and even enemy agents, attitudes embraced at several camps. Camp Funston was the worst. Forty objectors there were given draconian sentences for failing to follow mundane military orders, orders "framed," according to a later military report, for the very purpose of convicting them.[23]

Over the course of the next few months, the Wilson administration issued a series of orders modifying the treatment of objectors. On 25 September, Secretary of War Newton Baker wrote that Mennonites should not be "forced to wear uniforms as the question of raiment is one of the tenets of the faith." On the 10th of October he went further, recognizing the folly and the harm of intermixing objectors with men training as soldiers. Henceforth, objectors were to be segregated in camps and placed under the supervision of "specially selected" officers of "tact and consideration." Objectors' refusals to perform military tasks, subject to the Articles of War, were to be "quietly ignored." The army had received reports that treating objectors with "kindly consideration" worked. Treated in such manner, "men voluntarily removed their original exception to military service." The new order was not to be reported to the press. Treating objectors with "kindly consideration" was too controversial, even if it worked. Roosevelt's stentorian rhetoric was still to be feared.[24]

Were Baker's orders enforced? Not at Camp Funston. Soldiers beat Joseph Waldner so badly that he spent two weeks in hospital. Others forced Peter Tschetter to endure a mock execution. The physical abuse of Hutterites and some Mennonites for refusal to perform military duties continued well into 1918. In June of that year, soldiers beat and kicked nine Hutterites, forcing water down the throats of some, dragging another over a road freshly tarred and oiled.[25]

In December, the Wilson administration issued another confidential order that men who had "personal scruples against war" were to be treated the same as religious objectors. This was a reversal of Wilson's then personal belief in the spring of 1917, in response to a letter from John Nevin Sayre, whose brother was married to one of Wilson's daughters, that such a position would "open the door to so much that was unconscientious on the part of persons" seeking to avoid service. The animus against conscientious objectors stoked by Roosevelt and others constrained Wilson's policies. Yet here was a military directive affirming an ethical basis for conscientious objection years before the Supreme Court in 1965 made it the law of the land.[26]

Finally, in March 1918, the Wilson administration defined noncombatant service as service in the Medical and Quartermaster Corps or the Corps of Engineers. Prior to June 1918, roughly 1,500 men had chosen noncombatant service, among them dozens of Adventists whose testimonies reveal their diligent efforts to maintain their Sabbatarian principles. The same act reaffirmed that "conscientious scruples" independent of a religious sect or organization would qualify for noncombatant service, that objectors should continue to be segregated, and that they should face "no punitive hardship of any kind." Camp Funston, and perhaps others, ignored the latter message.[27]

In the end, Baker's liberal, albeit confidential, policies appear to have worked. A remarkable 80 percent of objectors gave up their claims and served under arms. One of them was Alvin York, the mountain marksman who became the celebrated hero of the war for killing some twenty-five German soldiers. At Camp Gordon, Georgia, his battalion commander, a fellow Christian and Harvard graduate, treated his beliefs with respect even as he argued that the Bible sanctioned war. York, allowed a home leave to consider his decision, came to a mountainside belief that God gave him "the assurance I needed" to go to war as a soldier. Historians have been skeptical of how common York's story was. "Some, no doubt, were persuaded by 'kindly considerations,'" David Kennedy wrote, "[b]ut others were humiliated and hazed, jeered and cajoled, until their consciences could accommodate war."[28]

In June, Baker established a Board of Inquiry consisting of three members whose job was to interview each of the remaining objectors and to make judgments on their dispositions. Their work was to be confidential—had it "been made public they might have been the means to create even more objectors." The Board had been given the authority to recommend alternative service—furloughs for farm or industrial work under stringent guidelines with respect to pay, as well as service with the Friends Reconstruction Unit in France. Two months earlier, Baker made clear that objectors who were "sullen and defiant" or whose "sincerity" was in question, or who were "active in propaganda should be promptly brought to trial by court martial."[29]

Of the roughly 4,000 objectors remaining in the camps, 1,300 elected to serve as noncombatants and another 1,300 to 1,500 chose work furloughs; 88 to 99 Quakers chose to work with the Friends Reconstruction Unit in France. Others who remained unassigned when the war ended would be sent home. Five hundred four had been court-martialed and imprisoned.[30]

These were the "absolutists." Some were Russian Molokans who refused any compromise with the military; others were Hutterite farmers who had the misfortune of being imprisoned before the introduction of farm furloughs, two of whom, Joseph and Michael Hofer, would die of pneumonia (or more likely influenza) after abusive confinement in a cold and wet dungeon. A larger number were well-educated objectors, men such as Evan Thomas, whose better known brother Norman regarded him as "prone to moral egotism."[31]

Evan Thomas did not believe the government had the authority to conscript him (the Supreme Court concluded otherwise). He refused both noncombatant service and a farm furlough. At his first camp, he captured the diversity of his fellow objectors with a certain condescension, "socialists of a not very intelligent type, two Seven Day Adventists with the most curious interpretations of the Bible, four typical colored brethren of a very courageous and devout sort—I like them—and one fellow who claims to be a great admirer of Nietzsche." At a later camp, he and his fellow objectors, according to a recent study of the Thomas family in these years, "disagreed about what they would do for the army, for themselves, and for each other." In a letter to his brother Norman, he wrote, "I can assure you that no men spent more time splitting hairs than we." In the end, Thomas elected to embrace a hunger strike that would lead to court-martial (after he refused to eat), a prison sentence where a refusal to work led to abusive treatment, and finally exoneration, eight months and a few weeks after his entry into the army.[32]

The Wilson administration's approach to conscientious objection was flawed from the start, failing to recognize the harassment objectors would face in training camps, failing to define the role of noncombatants for eleven months after the passage of the Draft Act, and failing to offer alternative service for objectors for more than a year. The army would make matters worse by trying men on minor and often "framed" charges of disobeying orders and sentencing them to absurdly long prison terms. Courts reduced such sentences. The last objectors walked free by November 1920.[33]

We may well honor the men who took absolutist positions, refusing both noncombatant assignments and farm furloughs. But having done that, they left the government no reasonable option but court-martial and conviction. Evan Thomas and others recognized that there is a cost to conscience, though his brother Norman would choose to insist that a just government should have honored the rights of absolutists. The British, who had similar policies on noncombatant and alternative service, sent more than 5,000 men who refused either option to prison. Canada offered no provision for alternative service. The Axis powers, as well as the French, refused to recognize any form of conscientious objection.[34]

There are other men worth honoring. One was an Adventist medic who volunteered to retrieve a wounded soldier who had "lain in a shell hole" for three nights in "no man's land." "Two other men had been trying to reach him, but failed," he testified, "as they said it was too dangerous a task." He and a buddy succeeded at bringing the man to safety while they were "constantly under shell and machine gun fire"—"the God of heaven kept us safe." Professing his willingness to do the same for "the sake of my fellow men," he concluded in a brief and modest account: "I received a French Croix de Guerre for bravery on the Soissons front." A picture of him with the award graces the frontispiece of a book whose author elected not to identify any of the young Adventists he interviewed.[35]

Then there is Richard L. Stierheim. He was working as a carpenter at the Sparrows Point steel works near Baltimore and drafted into the army sometime in 1918. He would claim to be opposed to war, but it is not clear that he ever made his claim before a draft board or told his commanding officer during training at Camp Meade. Once in France, however, he deserted. Captured near the Spanish border in September, he was convicted and sentenced to death. On the 3rd of November, near Verdun, he volunteered to rescue wounded men while under machine gun fire and continued to provide similar aid for nine days, volunteering for burial details and for litter duty both under heavy artillery fire. His commanding officer wrote, "I have never seen such bravery," urging clemency for his "conspicuous gallantry." Learning of Stierheim's bravery, General Pershing, the commander of all American troops in Europe, remitted his sentence of death and ordered him assigned as a noncombatant. Stierheim would live out his life as a carpenter outside Pittsburgh, raise a family, retire to Florida and die in 1966, the rare circumstances of his conscience and his bravery barely known.[36]

World War II
The Selective Training and Service Act of 1940 offered two significant

departures from its World War I counterpart. First, the Act broadened the definition of conscientious objection to include all those opposed to war by reason of "religious training and belief." Membership in a traditional peace church was no longer necessary. Yet the Act did not go as far as the Wilson administration's belated decision to acknowledge an ethical basis for conscientious objection. Second, it also provided for alternative service, defined as "work of national importance under civilian direction." Much of the credit for these departures rests with representatives of the traditional peace churches meeting with President Franklin Roosevelt in early 1940, later joined by other churches along with secular allies. They did not get all that they wanted. They had argued for the rights of absolutists, men who refused both noncombatant and alternative service, urging that the United States follow the British in now acknowledging such rights. No member of Congress spoke in favor.[37]

Some 72,000 men applied through their draft boards as objectors. They came from more than 230 churches and sects, a vast expansion from earlier years, though the majority—58 percent—were members of traditional peace churches. Only about 37,000 were actually drafted. Approximately 25,000 served as noncombatants, although the numbers may have been higher, while only 11,950 sought alternative service; 71 percent (6,980) were Mennonites, Brethren, or Friends. The one sect that faced special burdens was the Jehovah's Witnesses. They weren't technically conscientious objectors—they were prepared to fight at Armageddon—but the insistence that all Witnesses were ministers and thus entitled to ministerial exemption according to the Selective Service Act proved a hard sell to local draft boards. Though 532 Witnesses chose alternative service, more than 4,000 refused any compromise and went to jail.[38]

Lewis B. Hershey, the Director of the Selective Service from 1941 to 1970, and much maligned during the Vietnam War, was critical in ensuring that conscientious objectors were treated fairly and far better than they had been treated in World War I. Though not formally religious, Hershey was the descendant of Mennonites and was committed to the principle of conscientious objection as long as it entailed service to country. In 1941, he wrote to local boards: "It is general policy to show leniency in handling conscientious objectors and while regulations stipulate 'by reason of his religious training and belief,' such training might even be given in the home, and it is not necessary that a conscientious objector be a member of any recognized religious sect."[39]

It was Hershey who presided over the creation and oversight of the Civilian Public Service (CPS) program, an experiment making use of former New Deal Civilian Conservation Corps camps administered by peace church officials under the direction of Hershey's staff. The best that can be said for the program is that it established the statutory principle of alternative service for the future. The form, however, left much to be desired.[40]

The alternative service program was a makeshift experiment that seemed to satisfy no one. The peace church administrators, especially those from the Friends, found themselves in conflict with Selective Service officials, and Hershey chose to take full control of several camps. The objectors who toiled in the camps on soil conservation and forestry projects complained of meaningless make-work. Others served more usefully in mental hospitals. Veterans' organizations believed that objectors were being coddled, even though they received no federal pay or benefits and worked for the duration of the war, some working until 1947—the American Legion insisting that they not be demobilized faster than those who served in uniform. Some objectors volunteered for medical experiments that, however useful, fell far short of later ethical standards. Yet in the end, Hershey and the peace churches had devised a flawed solution that had come too late in World War I, permitting men who might otherwise have been jailed to serve as their consciences demanded.[41]

Initially noncombatant service, as in WWI, included service in the Corps of Engineers, and the Signal and Quartermaster Corps. But in January 1943, Secretary of War Henry Stimson decided that COs would in most cases be assigned to the Medical Corps. According to an authoritative account, objectors would thus train with other medics, receiving two weeks of basic military instruction without the use of weapons, followed by fifteen weeks of intensive medical training. Stimson's decision thus made it less likely that objectors would be exposed to the worst abuses of the World War I training camps, though we have no accounts of actual experience.[42]

Stimson's decision came too late for Desmond Doss. The first CO to be awarded the Medal of Honor, Doss was an Adventist from Lynchburg, Virginia. Entering the army in April 1942, he faced ugly peer pressure for two years, court-martial threats from his officers, efforts to transfer him, even to discharge him as unfit. He would earn the respect of his peers, first on Guam, then on Okinawa where for twelve hours he would toil under fire to lower wounded men ingeniously from the 350-foot Maeda Escarpment, misnamed Hacksaw Ridge in Oliver Stone's overwrought film. He paid a price, unmentioned in the film, of wounds to his left arm and the later loss of a lung leading to 100 percent disability. It would not keep him from appearing before President Harry Truman, who placed the Medal of Honor around his neck.[43]

Doss preferred to be known as a conscientious cooperator. Carlyle B. Haynes of the Adventists' War Service Commission popularized the term in the years before World War II. It was an effort, as he later explained, to draw a sharp distinction between the Adventists and the traditional peace churches. "We despise the term 'conscientious objector,'" he said, "and we despise the philosophy back of it.... We are not pacifists, and we believe in force for justice's sake, but a Seventh-day Adventist cannot take human life." In keeping with an ethic of cooperation with the American government and military, Haynes and others were enthusiastic supporters of the Medical Cadet Corps (MCC) which became widespread on Adventist college campuses in the 1940s. The MCC's purpose was to train young Adventist men in military discipline and battlefield first aid in preparation for their service in the military.[44]

Doss was one of 12,000 Adventists who served as noncombatants, almost half of those who were so designated by their draft boards. Most served in anonymity, though medic Orville Cox would be awarded a Silver Star for gallantry on Guadalcanal and a second award for his actions on Luzon, and Duane Kinman would achieve fame as a "foxhole surgeon," for performing an emergency tracheotomy with his jackknife.[45]

With the exception of the actor Lew Ayres, we know little about noncombatant objectors from other religions. Ayres, who gained fame for his leading role in the American version of *All Quiet on the Western Front*, was a self-taught seeker (he had never finished high school) who, according to a member of his draft board, had "a kind of religion of his own." He wanted to serve in the Medical Corps, but his draft board assigned him instead to a Civilian Public Service (CPS) camp in Oregon. His prominence provoked intense public controversy leading to the banning of his films in several cities. Yet there was also public support for him, and with the intervention of General Hershey he gained his wish. He enlisted in the Medical Corps and served for twenty-two months in the Pacific as a chaplain's assistant and hospital medic, returning with three battle stars, marking landings in Hollandia, Luzon, and Leyte.[46]

Doss, Cox, Ayres and so many others honored their consciences while risking their lives as a result of their willingness to serve. An anonymous noncombatant offered a deeply thoughtful weighing of the choices he faced: "It is practically impossible to avoid complicity with the war effort … even the man in prison probably contributes thru the products of his work; there are two scales to be balanced—the degree of participation in the destruction and the degree of activity in constructive work, in prison and in C.P.S., while there is little of the former, there is also very little opportunity for significant alternative service; in [noncombatant service] there is a closer participation in the warfare, but the opportunities for a ministry of goodwill are much greater and more needed."[47]

Toward the Vietnam War

The war in Europe ended in 1945, but the draft continued despite growing popular opposition. The military needed new troops for occupation duty because it was facing intense anger, to the point of rioting, among war-weary troops demanding to be sent home. Scheduled to end in May 1946, the draft survived until the spring of 1947 when, with the support of President Harry Truman, it ended. It was premature. The pressures of the impending Cold War led to the draft's reinstatement in June 1948. The Selective Service Act of that year, with its classifications for conscientious objectors (1-0 for alternative service, 1-A-0 for noncombatant service) would remain in place through the end of the Vietnam War.[48]

There is little written about conscientious objection during the Korean

War, and even less about those who served as noncombatants. A singular legal case affords evidence of an Adventist, James Girouard, seeking both citizenship and the opportunity to serve as a noncombatant. The Bureau of Naturalization denied his citizenship request because he answered no to the question would he bear arms if called upon to do so. The Supreme Court, however, decided in his favor, leading to a rewrite of the Bureau's questionnaire allowing for conscientious objection.[49]

From 1954 to the end of the American war in Vietnam, uniformed conscientious objectors experienced significant change. In that year, the army opened, for the first time, a dedicated basic training facility for conscientious objectors at Fort Sam Houston in San Antonio, Texas. Echo Company, 4th Battalion, located in the "Long Barracks" built in the 1870s, was home to CO basic training for seventeen years until the end of the draft. In that same year the SDA church began a partnership with the Army Medical Corps which encouraged Adventist COs in basic training to volunteer for human trials of vaccines and antibiotics for certain disabling bacteriological agents. It came to be known as "Operation Whitecoat." The decision to send American ground troops to Vietnam resulted in increased draft calls from 1965 on. Growing opposition to the war would dramatically increase the numbers of COs, especially those seeking alternative service. And finally two Supreme Court decisions would fundamentally alter what it meant to be a "religious" conscientious objector.[50]

Basic training at Fort Sam Houston consisted of six weeks of drill, physical training, compass and infiltration courses, the use of gas masks, as well as classes on military history and military courtesy—the army's standard training minus the rifle range. (In my memory, we were treated by most of the training cadre, many of whom were Latino, with respectful care. We weren't, after all, standard army recruits. COs could be prickly. There was little abuse and, in deference to the religious beliefs of most, there was no abusive language. The Viet Cong were neither demonized nor racialized. We were taught to respect and fear them, as in "Victor Charles gonna sneak up and do a number on you." The mess hall had won several awards and offered vegetarian fare to the Adventists. This was not Hollywood's version of basic training).[51]

At graduation, COs moved across post to begin ten weeks of medical training where they were a small minority alongside men who had graduated from the army's standard basic training. Since no one shouldered arms in medical training, COs could be anonymous if they so chose. Trainees learned how to clear an airway, apply a splint and a tourniquet, how to use the plastic packaging on a field dressing to treat a sucking chest wound, how to perform a cricothyroidotomy—and why that was safer than a tracheotomy—as well as how to draw blood, give shots, and recognize the symptoms of typhus and malaria. In a final field training exercise, in place as late as 1969, they learned how to evacuate wounded on stretchers from a set piece battlefield and carry them to a nearby aid station—training more suited to World War II than to a jungle war with few set piece battles, fewer stretchers in the field, and no aid stations in walking distance. The need for medics in Vietnam was overwhelming—every infantry platoon, consisting of thirty soldiers, went into combat with a medic while many more medics staffed aid stations on fire bases and landing zones.

Operation Whitecoat found its home at Fort Detrick, Maryland. During World War II, Camp Detrick, as it was then known, became a center for learning how to establish medical defenses against infectious diseases as well as organisms deployed for biological warfare. Fort Detrick, however, was also a center for the offensive use of chemical and biological weapons and would remain so until 1969 when then President Richard Nixon banned such research and development. Operation Whitecoat became controversial in the late 1960s both within the SDA church and especially outside it. Major newspapers and magazines, *The New York Times*, *The Washington Post*, and *The New Republic* among them, and broadcasters NBC and CBS, offered critical looks at the use of human volunteers (human "guinea pigs") in medical experiments. Seymour Hersh in a brief article in *Ramparts* suggested that SDA leadership was "naive" in its belief that young Adventists were not being used to test offensive chemical weapons. Yet he offered no evidence that they were.[52]

Now some fifty years later, it seems clear that Operation Whitecoat was what it was intended to be, a program to develop vaccines and antibiotics for such diseases as Q fever, tularemia, and encephalitis, among others.

Young Adventist men who were vegetarians and did not smoke or drink were an ideal medical pool for such experiments. They were chosen twice a year after visits to basic training overseen by representatives of the Medical Corps and the SDA Church. Not everyone who volunteered was selected. It appears that men who had some college were preferred. Officially they were volunteers twice over. After volunteering to be in the program, they also had to volunteer for specific experiments. There is anecdotal evidence that some 20 percent of men went through the two-year program without volunteering for any experiments. Experiments made men sick, some seriously. None died. A 2005 study of 522 former Whitecoats (roughly a quarter of the 2,300 who served) found that 87 percent reported their health as good or excellent. While some reported elevated cases of asthma and headache, the report concluded there was "no adverse impact on the overall health" of the respondents who had once served as Whitecoats.[53]

Yet the idea of human guinea pigs still promotes a questioning unease. In a largely positive 2003 PBS report on the 30-year reunion of former Whitecoats (they are the only COs who have such reunions), the audience heard that very phrase repeated. There remains much that is unknown. How well-policed were the borders between defensive biochemical experiments and their offensive use? Why didn't the army offer blood tests to the respondents in the 2005 study? Why has there been no study of those Whitecoats who died? A small minority of former Whitecoats continue to claim long-term disability. One is Gene Crosby, who has suffered two heart attacks, a stroke, and now has an autoimmune disease. Rhonda Crosby tells us that Gene's brother, a medic in Germany, warned him about the risks of serving as a medic in Vietnam: "Gene took the chance to stay alive" stateside. He "is wishing now that he took the chance" to go to war.[54]

During the years of the Vietnam War, Operation Whitecoat was a ticket to "stay alive." Operation Whitecoat may have remained the same program from 1954 to 1973, but after 1965 it took on a different meaning. Now large numbers of Adventists, overwhelming majorities, chose to volunteer during the two cycles of basic training per year when army doctors and SDA leaders came to make their selections. One Adventist, whom I interviewed, timed his induction (yes, you could volunteer for induction) to ensure that he would be in basic training during a selection visit. He had researched the process. The presence of Adventist leaders during the selection process could pose conflicts of interest, favoring the sons of leaders, ministers, and congregants known to such leaders. In a later chapter, Tom Hirst will give voice to that suspicion. Hirst volunteered for Whitecoat but was not selected. He had a reputation, he believed, as a less-than-faithful Adventist and he was well known to one of the elders who took part in the interviews.[55]

That same year—1965—also marked the beginnings of a change in the legal definition of conscientious objection. Prior to 1965, the men who passed through the Long Barracks were overwhelmingly religious. Roughly half were Seventh-day Adventists, just as they had been in World War II. The other half came not just from the traditional peace churches but from a great variety of religious faiths, again just as they had in World War II. Roman Catholics, Missouri Synod Lutherans, Eastern Orthodox, Baptists, Methodists, Episcopalians, Bahá'í, and many others professed their willingness to serve but not to kill. They had to make their case in writing and sometimes in person before their local draft boards. They had to profess their opposition to killing in all wars. The Selective Service System did not recognize a right to selective conscientious objection. And prior to 1965, they had to make their case grounded in "religious training and belief." In that year the Supreme Court, in *United States v. Seeger*, broadened the definition of "religious training and belief" to include beliefs "that occupy the same place . . . as the belief in a traditional deity." In 1970, the Supreme Court went even farther in *Welsh v. United States* when it explicitly allowed "moral and ethical beliefs" to be sufficient grounds for conscientious objection.[56]

Conscientious objection increased over the course of the Vietnam War as opposition to the war grew, and it would appear that it increased even more sharply in the wake of the *Welsh* decision. Between 1963 and 1972, conscientious objectors comprised 4.13 percent of all those who were inducted. The comparable number for World War II was a minuscule .38 percent. Stephen M. Kohn documented the steep increase in the ratio of CO exemptions to inductions after 1970. John Whiteclay Chambers noted the remarkable fact that in 1972 there were more men classified as COs than were inducted into the army.[57]

With the end of the draft, the era of the CO medic was over. Yet conscientious objection survived for those in service. During the buildup to Operation Desert Storm (1991), some 1,000 to 2,000 or more men and women filed as conscientious objectors. They attracted considerable publicity and some surprising Congressional sympathy—given the natural skepticism about the timing of their claims—in the passage of the Military Conscientious Objector Act of 1992, an effort to reform the process for in-service objectors. The Department of Defense reported a 73 percent approval rate for the years 1988 to 1991. Only 16 percent of army applicants and 11 percent of Marine applicants requested noncombatant service. Unless army applicants had prior medical training, none would have served as medics. The Afghanistan and Iraq war never saw such concentrated numbers nor the publicity that Desert Storm elicited. Between 2002 and 2006 there were roughly 100 cases per year. About half were approved.[58]

The era of the CO medic going to war may well be over, but it should not be forgotten. From the beginning of World War II to the end of the Vietnam War, COs willing to serve made their claims before local draft boards and trained as medics. Most went to war. What follows is the story of some of those who served in the Vietnam War.

CHAPTER 2

A California Pantheist

In 1965, the Supreme Court in *United States v. Seeger* broadened the definition of "religious training and belief" to include "a sincere and meaningful belief which occupies in the life of its possessor a place parallel to that filled by the God of those admittedly qualifying for the [conscientious objection] exemption." And so "Buddhists, Confucians, and Taoists," and perhaps even pantheists and moralists, could now successfully claim to be conscientious objectors. It would take time for local draft boards to absorb the lessons of *United States v. Seeger*. It was not until the war in Vietnam was winding down, and the end of the draft was imminent, that the full effects of *Seeger* became manifest. When I went through basic training in the summer of 1969, I was surrounded by men who came to their beliefs in the traditional religious way. But the door was now open, and John Hubenthal would walk through it.[1]

John Hubenthal served as a 19-year-old conscientious objector medic in the 1st Battalion, 327th Infantry Regiment, 101st Airborne Division for fourteen months from 1969 to 1970, assigned first to a line infantry company, then to a reconnaissance platoon, ending his tour as a member of a Civil Action Team. Awarded the Bronze Star for Valor, he estimated that he treated the battlefield wounds of forty to fifty soldiers. Suffering from a cancer, diagnosed in late 2004, that affected his speech, he sat down to a series of telephone interviews as part of the oral history program of Texas Tech University's Vietnam Center. The interviews spanned the weeks between

CHAPTER 2

December 2005 and February 2006.²

He would live only a few months more, dying at the age of 56 on 3 September 2006 in Newton, Massachusetts. His wife Wendy had first contacted Texas Tech. She had been a facilitator in a course at the University of Massachusetts Boston on therapeutic autobiography in 2003–2004. The interviews afforded John a form of final reckoning with the pain and the pride of his service.³

The transcript reveals a man facing death struggling to talk and struggling with memory. He made clear that he was recounting memories, in some cases, against the grain of a "thirty-year" effort "to wipe those tapes" of memory clean. "I worked on forgetting," he said—an effort that can lead and has led to distorted memory for Vietnam veterans. His memory, he said, was marked by an inability to "forget the details, they're hardwired," as if "burned on to a disc," while also claiming that "accurate chronology comes hard." He continued: "I didn't want to remember. It was bloody and terrifying and ghastly. I didn't want to hang on to that stuff. So there are going to be voids."⁴

He "worked on forgetting" and yet he can't "forget the details." The problem of memory for those struggling with PTSD was ably summarized by David Morris in his *The Evil Hours*: "Chief among the crimes that trauma commits against the mind is the distortions of memory it produces ... mind skips straight over some things and perversely over-records others." As Hubenthal acknowledged, his is a fragile, partial, and, at times, contradictory memory and, despite his claims that he cannot forget the details, his readers cannot fully trust it.⁵

He relates stories from his basic training of two trainees walking sentry who were victims of "drive-by shootings," an anachronistic phrase, while a few moments later, admitting his knowledge came from "barracks talk ... scuttlebutt," but then asserting that at least one of these shootings happened to a trainee in a medical training cycle "ahead of me." But he could not have witnessed it. He would go on to relate a story of his first days in Vietnam of soldiers playing games with live hand grenades that strains belief, and that may well be unique in reportage on the war.[6]

He would tell another far more disturbing story about "Fuzzy," a member of his recon platoon in the 1st of the 327th, who wore a necklace of Vietnamese ears. Cutting the ears off an enemy soldier, or a Vietnamese villager, is a war crime. The story bears an ugly resemblance to that of a similar soldier who two years earlier in the same recon unit was at the center of a series of war crimes. Was Fuzzy real, or did such stories continue to circulate in the recon platoon of the 1st of the 327th? Hubenthal regarded Fuzzy not as a war criminal but as "a highly admirable character," raising an even more difficult question about his moral judgment.[7]

His voice in these interviews is often thoughtful and introspective, at times sardonic and playful, more than once indulging in adolescent humor. It is also the voice of a man who only belatedly has come to understand himself. It wasn't until he was in his fifties that he learned that he suffered from both attention deficit disorder (ADD) and PTSD. He was dismissive of his ADD diagnosis; he believed he simply learned differently than others and, despite a checkered post-Vietnam employment history, he would eventually earn a PhD and teach at the New Hampshire Institute of Art.[8]

Returning home from Vietnam, he wanted to put the war behind him. He did not want to be defined by his service: "I'm not one of these people walking around with buttons and my old cammies," though in later life he drove a car with a Bronze Star license plate (it kept him from getting parking tickets, he said). He mentioned that he had joined Vietnam Veterans Against the War (VVAW) but was not active. He had little contact with other veterans, or with the men with whom he served. Yet his memories continued to intrude.[9]

There were triggers that would lead to weeping. He never knew where they would come from. He compared himself perhaps fittingly to the Kurt Vonnegut character Billy Pilgrim, an unreliable narrator in *Slaughterhouse-Five*, becoming "unstuck in time." "I'm cruising down a freeway and all of a sudden I'm weeping hysterically. I'm listening to machine guns and helicopters. I'm smelling the jungle." There was a period of years when he could not listen to the Joni Mitchell album *Blue*. The sounds of guns or firecrackers caused him to leap through a door, and "I don't bother to open it." Though he quickly clarified: It was only a window with a screen he leapt through, doing some damage to the plants below. He had learned no better account for his reactions than the World War I explanation of "shellshock," though in a more contemporary register, he admitted that his friends saw him as the "crazy" Vietnam vet: "There goes John again." Over time, the symptoms lessened, but we never learn what led him to seek treatment, if that is what he did, or how he came to be diagnosed with what he called "long-term" PTSD.[10]

We should honor his service as a man who made a conscience-driven choice to serve in Vietnam on his own moral terms. Yet we cannot expect him to be the master of his memory, nor can we ignore his troubling respect for Fuzzy. His end-of-life narrative, spoken over a phone to a stranger, offers moments of blunt honesty, the customary bravado of aging veterans with war stories to tell, and the flawed memory of a man who admittedly wanted to erase it all.

For many men and women ably informed by lazy journalists and filmmakers, war trauma leads directly to PTSD. This is oversimple to scholars of the subject. PTSD was not something that was "discovered" by "astute clinicians," according to Richard J. McNally, a leading scholar, who leans toward the view that it was a "socially constructed artifact of the Vietnam War," helping to explain and giving a name to a bundle of symptoms, "nightmares, anxiety, hypervigilance, irritability and emotional disconnection" common to some returning veterans. Allan Young went further, arguing that PTSD was "invented"—"glued together by the practices, technologies, and narratives with which it is diagnosed, studied, treated, and represented and by the various interests, institutions, and moral arguments that mobilized those efforts and resources." None of this is meant to suggest that some of the underlying issues veterans faced weren't real. I recall dreading the sound of helicopters, and once, on a hike in New Hampshire, obsessively imagining the possible locations of ambushes. PTSD gave it a name, and for some veterans it offered a form of narrative closure, an explanation for some others of a troubled postwar life.[11]

Another popular conceit is that war trauma pervasively haunts veterans. A study from 1988 claimed that 30.9 percent of male veterans had developed PTSD and that 15.2 percent still had it at the time of the study. A subsequent study from 2006, using the same data, found 18.7 percent had developed it and 9.1 percent still had it as of the date of the first study. It matters how you define impairment and what the "threshold" is in order to classify someone as having PTSD, according to McNally. A stricter definition of "functional impairment," again according to McNally, would have reduced those numbers to the single digits with just 5.4 percent still suffering as of the late 1980s. The 2006 study made clear that the majority of combat veterans never suffered PTSD, that the functioning of veterans who once had PTSD was little different from those who never had it, and that a majority of those who once had it were never treated for it, indicating that personal resilience may have a greater impact. A recent scholarly study suggests just that. The majority of trauma victims, not just veterans, never develop PTSD. It turns out we know far more about PTSD than we know about resilience. Would a different framing focused on resilience, manifested by his earned PhD and his teaching career, have led to a different life narrative for John Hubenthal?[12]

Born in Long Beach, California, in 1950 into an upper middle-class family, his father was a navy officer in World War II and later the CEO of a company that built cooling towers, a supporter of Richard Nixon in 1968 and a supporter of the war. His mother was an art major from UCLA and a "dyed-in-the-wool New Deal Democrat." His early politics more closely tracked those of his mother.[13]

He was drawn to the '60s counterculture, its folk music, its antiwar vibe, and the lure of sex, drugs, and rock and roll. At 15 he joined a peace group at Ventura Community College; at 16, he joined Students for a Democratic Society. He was educated, not in school, where he admitted he had been a poor student, but by the counterculture and peace movements. Everything he learned about the war came from peace movement handouts. He came to see himself as a "revolutionary," though one distinctly in the American grain. Years later, he would claim that he had resisted the temptation to "go party-line knee jerk," that is, as he explained, to embrace the idea that

"America is the source of all evil in the world." He could not get through Marx's *Das Kapital*. His lodestars were Thomas Paine and, especially, Henry David Thoreau. He wrote poetry and admired Walt Whitman and would come to carry a copy of *Leaves of Grass* in his Vietnam rucksack.[14]

The draft loomed when he graduated from high school in 1968. He had no interest in college. Oddly, given his earlier history, he claimed he had lost his habit of reading, except for his own poetry, his "beloved Thoreau," and comic books. All he knew about the war in Vietnam came from the antiwar movement and from "the news." When asked what he was thinking about his impending draft, he offered three answers: first, the bravado of "they're not going to get me"; second, a "how dare they do this?" sense of "universalized outrage" that marked the experience of so many on the antiwar left; and third, a more personal plea: "I don't want to go off and get shot."[15]

And then the oddest of twists. He decided he wanted to go to war. His then girlfriend dissented. He told her we were getting much more civilized: "This is maybe the last chance anybody will have to see what war is all about." He could only explain it to his interviewer as a form of "thrill seeking," the equivalent of driving a car faster than he should. We need to remember he was only 18, but then in his 50s he can only explain his decision as "thrill seeking."[16]

And then another twist. He was willing to serve but not willing to kill. His decision to seek 1-A-0 status was unusual to the point of bizarre. His objection to the war was political, and in the long interview that forms the basis of all we know about him, he never alluded to a conventional religious background. His memorial service at a Unitarian church in Newton, Massachusetts, underscored it.[17]

He told his draft board that he was a pantheist, likely inspired in part by his reading of Thoreau, that "God is in everything and so killing is necessarily immoral." A Southern California draft board bought it and, according to his account, without even interviewing him. However, because he had been arrested for pot possession, he had to await an investigation into his moral fitness to serve in the army.[18]

During the six-month hiatus while he waited for the army's decision on his fitness to serve, he lived a picaresque existence in San Francisco, settling into a condemned squat with his girlfriend and assorted hippies, dog breeders, and a woman who was a banker by day, a prostitute by night, supporting himself by hawking the *Berkeley Barb*, the famed alternative paper, reading and writing poetry. He read Whitman along with the Russian dissidents, Anna Akhmatova and Yevgeny Yevtushenko, and wrote in the tradition of Sandburg. Offered a reading at City Lights, the well-known bookstore of Lawrence Ferlinghetti, he opted at the last minute not to go on, feeling that his poems were a poor fit with the obscure stream of consciousness rambles that preceded him. Asked if he had kept his poems, he answered no, "I'm not much of a keeper, I'm sorry to say."[19]

He did recall a single poem he remembered with some pride.

> The rose I gave you is still there on the dashboard
> Made of silk and plastic shaped with heat and glue
> It looks like a real one but it will last forever
> Smell industrial only ruined by the dew.

It's best that he found other outlets for his talents.[20]

He returned home and asked his draft board to speed his induction. He began basic training at Fort Sam Houston in January 1969. He saw himself, and his fellow COs, as the "pariahs of the military," and the drill instructors and officers who oversaw his training as men who must have done something wrong to merit such an assignment. His experience mirrors that of many other COs. His drill instructors lived up to their harsh stereotypes, but "nobody got smacked around." He noted that they were wary of the troubles that conscience-driven CO trainees might bring, yet he also recalled a meeting in medical training with a former drill instructor who was pursuing an MA in psychology to better understand the nature of his work.[21]

During his time in basic training, he remembered that there were as many as three "companies," classes actually (there was only one basic training company), training at the same time, their starting dates staggered, each with their own barracks and latrines, the latter decorated with murals painted by former trainees extolling the virtues of CO medics: "No guns, sir, just guts," as he recalled the caption.[22]

He also reported that CO basic training included a class in hand-to-hand combat, where he claimed he was taught how to "kill people with your bare hands." He elaborated. You grabbed your victim by the neck from behind, then threw your body backward. His interviewer never questioned why a hand-to-hand killing technique would be taught to men opposed to killing. In my experience, classes in hand-to-hand combat were optional. I opted in. What we learned was purely defensive, and as if to underscore the training's likely ineffectuality, a young Latino sergeant made clear that if any of us were involved in scuffles on the streets of San Antonio we had no reason to expect that our brief training would allow us to prevail.[23]

His class was overwhelmingly white. He remembered the sharp divide between middle and upper middle-class COs—"counterculture type people"—like himself and poorer and less educated "Bible Belt" fundamentalists. Otherwise, he had no distinct memory of the religious beliefs of those like himself. His memory of the cultural divide in his class was, however, flawed or perhaps he never understood it at the time. Some in his class volunteered for the Whitecoat program, a program of medical experimentation he regarded as sinister: "some weird Nazi Germany scene." He had no idea where they went or what happened to them, nor could he identify them as Seventh-day Adventists. The men chosen for the program he remembered had to be "pure in body and soul," no alcohol, tobacco, caffeine—"snake-handlers' dietary practices," he remarked derisively.[24]

After completing basic training, he moved across post to begin his medical training. He was harshly critical. The training "was wildly, totally, completely inadequate for the job I was assigned to. If I had been assigned to be a hospital orderly it would have been perfect. I learned bedpans. I learned how to change sheets without taking the patient out [of the bed]. . . . Hospital stuff, basically. We had some emergency first aid sort of stuff but hardly up to the level of even a civilian EMT." Medical training was a "factory," he and his fellow trainees were "product." "They were cranking us out." No one failed: "Washing out was not an option."[25]

Few of his trainers were veterans of the Vietnam War, and he learned little about what he would soon face. "They didn't teach us anything about jungle rot. They didn't teach us anything about lancing boils. They didn't teach us anything about the varieties of rashes or what you do with FUOs [fevers of unknown origin] or how—they didn't teach us anything about jungle medicine, field jungle medicine, and they taught us damned little about how you deal with combat injuries. Most of what I learned, most of what I did as a medic, I taught myself once I got there. Once I realized that I was in way over my head and that I had a serious job to do that the army hadn't prepared me for."[26]

This resonates with my own experience. In a final two-day exercise in the foothills of South Texas in the fall of 1969, I learned how to evacuate wounded soldiers from a set piece battlefield, carrying them on stretchers to an aid station just behind the lines. In Vietnam, there were no set piece battle lines, no stretchers in the field, and no aid stations in walking distance. Four years into an intense jungle war, the Army Medical Corps inexcusably trained medics for World War II. Most of what I learned as a medic, I learned in Vietnam.[27]

Hubenthal arrived in Vietnam in the spring of 1969 assigned to 3rd Platoon, Delta Company, 1st of 327th, 101st Airborne Division. It was by his account a dysfunctional platoon. The platoon leader and the platoon sergeant were at odds. He had heard of a fragging incident. None of this should be surprising. In the post-Vietnamization army, morale eroded—no one wanted to be the last man to die as increasing numbers of Army and Marine units rotated home. Yet his account of a night spent on a forward observation post is uniquely bizarre and difficult to believe.[28]

He accompanied four soldiers that night, all of whom he believed had been involved in the fragging incident, though after more pointed questioning, he admitted he heard no admissions of guilt, "just vague references."

"All these guys," he said, "were short timers. They were down to a month or less and they were mad as hatters and just didn't give a shit anymore." They brought with them "giant bags of pot."²⁹

Let him tell the story: "These guys obviously got a live one with me. I've been there ten days or less, eight days or less. Couldn't find my asshole with both hands and a flashlight, basically. And once they found out that I had come over intentionally with no weapon I was the most wonderful toy they'd ever had to play with. 'You did what? You're the craziest motherfucker I ever met in my life! What the hell?' And that's where it started and sort of went on all night. Obviously, I did not sleep all night."³⁰

His fellow soldiers spent the night "throwing hand grenades back at their own perimeter, screaming obscenities at their lieutenant, and firing bursts at random all around them just for the hell of it. 'What are you going to do when you get into combat?' one of them asked. I said, 'Well, I'm a medic. I'll take care of the wounded.' 'Well, what are you going to do if you have to fight?' 'To tell you the truth, I haven't thought about it.' They said, 'Well you might start thinking about it.' Pulled the pin, pop spoon, threw a live hand grenade in my lap." "Nobody moved," he said, they just "laughed." He responded quickly and threw the live grenade far enough away so that no one was wounded. He heard the explosion. In order to believe such a story we must also believe that four soldiers were willing to put their own lives at risk in order to invigilate a "cherry" CO medic.³¹

A few days later, he saw his first combat. Ambushed at night, he heard the call medic. Twice he responded, walking upright to the wounded soldiers; "nobody had taught me how to move," he said. Twice fellow soldiers threw him to the ground. After successfully treating his two comrades, he claimed that "my commitment to being a CO collapsed." He picked up an M16.³²

A few weeks later, he took part in a battalion-level airmobile assault in the A Shau Valley. The landing zone was hot. Under fire he leapt from a helicopter that he believed later crashed. He recalled rounds just missing his left and then his right shoulders. He treated a casualty, a soldier with a chest wound, dragging him first to relative safety. At this point in the interview, he was struggling with "nightmare snapshots" of memory. He spent the night dealing with the wounded, one man dying in his arms.

His platoon commander was dead; he recalled that only six of thirty of his platoon members had survived.[33]

Covered with blood, he remembered being slapped awake at first light by a fellow soldier who may have thought him dead. His company commander then "walks up to me with what looks like a stick with mud caked on it. It was the rifle I'd been carrying and he's holding it by the barrel like it was a bag of shit. He's looking at this thing and he looks at me and he says, 'Doc, is this yours?' I didn't even think about it. I said, 'Not anymore.' I got no use for that thing. I was very fortunate that he was a good officer because he could literally have shot me right there."

No, he could not have, and Hubenthal seemed to acknowledge that as he clumsily qualified his assertion—refusing to take up your rifle was "only a court-martial offense," and his captain knew he was a CO. The trauma of the event and of his memory of it still weighed on him. He never carried a weapon again.[34]

He remained in the field as his company moved from patrolling near the Laotian border and then east to Phú Thọ Province south of Huế—a mistake of memory or possibly transcription. The province south of Huế was known as Thừa Thiên during the time of the war. Phú Thọ was a province in the north. He had been promoted to E-5 and now served as the company medic. An argument with a senior NCO about who should or should not be medevacked ultimately led to a reassignment to Echo Company's recon platoon where he learned a new skill—demolition. He came to carry a block of C-4, a plastic explosive, in his pack. His rationale was both bizarre and mordant. He didn't want to come home "light," that is missing an arm or leg or something even more valuable. "I'd rather join the red-haze brigade," he said. "I wasn't carrying a weapon but, by God, shoot me and I'll get your ass anyway." Maybe it was just bravado, but he didn't seem to understand that carrying that much C-4 posed a greater risk to his fellow soldiers than to the enemy.[35]

He did seem to understand the madness. "What was happening is I was going crazy because everybody who goes through that experience is nuts. And I mean clinically put them in a box, man. You know? Get the net. You know? It's an insane environment and it always has been."[36]

CHAPTER 2

Then another disturbing tale. Hubenthal's story about "Fuzzy," a member of his recon platoon, bears a remarkable resemblance to one that happened two years earlier in the same recon platoon, a war crime account uncovered by two reporters for the *Toledo Blade* in 2004. First Fuzzy's story. Fuzzy was a Chicano who, according to Hubenthal, had been in Vietnam for "at least four tours, nonstop." Fuzzy was "seriously dangerous" and did a lot of "freelance work." "He used to wear a necklace of left ears, about sixteen or seventeen of them, and they were all his. You know, it's not like he was picking them up. Certified kills. Every one. Probably in the dark, alone, on his own." Certified kills . . . in the dark, alone, on his own? What is the likelihood that the VC or the NVA would be so inept at protecting their perimeter? Far more likely was that Fuzzy was killing Vietnamese peasants who may or may not have been VC sympathizers. Hubenthal considered Fuzzy a friend: "If anybody would get me out of a jam if one came up he was the guy," an understandable assertion. Far less understandable was Hubenthal's belief that a man guilty of war crimes—the violation of enemy corpses is a violation of the Geneva Conventions—was "a highly admirable character."[37]

Fuzzy and Hubenthal were members of the recon platoon of the 1st of 327th, a unit that had been known as Tiger Force, a "Raider-like unit," since it had been formed in 1965 when then Maj. David Hackworth was the battalion executive officer. They would wear distinctive "tiger suits," camouflaged fatigues (recall Hubenthal's comment about his choice not to wear his "cammies" as a mark of his service). The Tigers, according to Hackworth, would offer the battalion a "long-range reconnaissance and ambush element *that would operate independently*" (italics added).[38]

In 2004, two reporters from the *Toledo Blade* would write a story, based on a cache of records saved by Col. Henry Tufts, that Tiger Force committed a staggering number of war crimes from May through November 1967 in an area south of Đà Nẵng, crimes that would never be adjudicated. They won a Pulitzer for their reporting and expanded on it in the publication of *Tiger Force: A True Story of Men and War* in 2006. One of their conclusions is that Tiger Force had operated far too "independently."[39]

Sam Ybarra became the face of Tiger Force. The child of a Mexican

American and a Navajo, he grew up in Globe, Arizona. Arrested frequently for disorderly conduct and underage drinking, he enlisted in the army and became a member of Tiger Force in early 1967. He was a loner, frequently walking point, and at least once, leaving his night defensive position and returning at dawn with a scalp. Ybarra, according to multiple witnesses, assembled a collection of ears, openly wore ear necklaces, throwing them away when the stink got too great, replacing them with ears he carried in a "ration bag filled with vinegar." He also slit the throat of a defenseless villager, and cut off the head of a child. Dying at the age of 36 from cirrhosis of the liver, the result of drinking to forget, Sam Ybarra paid a price for his barbarous behavior.[40]

Sam Ybarra was not "Fuzzy." Ybarra served two years earlier than Hubenthal's Fuzzy—a Chicano slipping out at night, returning with ears, wearing an ear necklace. The cutting of ears by soldiers and Marines in Vietnam is well established; the wearing of ear necklaces was less well established. *Tiger Force* provides, however, a multiply attested confirmation of the wearing of ear necklaces. We are left with two choices. Either a veteran with a troubled memory invented "Fuzzy," channeling the war stories Tiger Force's soldiers once told about Sam Ybarra, or Fuzzy was real and Tiger Force continued at a minimum to cut and collect ears. In either case, we are left with the disturbing conclusion that Hubenthal found a man who mutilated bodies "admirable."

Whatever questions we might have about his memory or his lapse in moral judgment, John Hubenthal's gift to posterity is his long interview voiced just a few months before his death. The transcript makes clear that there were times when talking was painful for him. But talk he did, offering us the story of an unusual, pantheist path to CO status. He overcame his first stumbling attempts to treat wounded soldiers and came to take great pride in his medical skills. "I took care of my guys. . . . I had sutures. I had iodine gauze. I had a full minor surgical kit. And I knew what to do. I knew how to lance a boil and pack it. I knew how to deal with extreme jungle rot and I'd fight for them. I'd get them in the rear if they needed to be there. You know? So I was a valuable commodity, and the guys knew this."[41]

In reflecting on his decision to serve as a CO, he called himself an "old-fashioned patriot," "a real whole-hearted participant in this American Revolution thing." He was proud and grateful that he "lived in the one country that would let me serve honorably without compromising my beliefs"—the one country claim an exaggeration, but testament to a personal moral decision that became a "life-long source of really patriotic pride." Asked if he ever considered going to Canada, he answered, "Not a thought. Never crossed my mind. This is my country."[42]

CHAPTER 3

A Roman Catholic from New Jersey

David Rogers's story as a CO medic is singular. He came to serve from a sense of community responsibility—if he didn't go, someone else would go in his place. He never carried a weapon, yet he returned with an intense feeling of guilt for his complicity in the war. He would go on to a career as a distinguished journalist and was able to publicly reflect on the meaning of the war.

"Sometimes, it's just like *Lord of the Flies* out there. Eleven bushes are wonderful people [11B is the army designation for an infantryman], but this is a very corrupting experience. Everyone is young here now. Some guys get weird at times. They don't want me to dustoff [medevac] a wounded VC. They say they want to see him die. Then other times we'll run into some other unit of Americans, and I'll start throwing flowers and leaves at them and these same guys will join in."[1]

David Rogers, a conscientious objector (CO) medic in the 1st Infantry Division who had suffered a scalp wound a few days earlier, was being interviewed by James P. Sterba for *The New York Times* in November 1969. The Sterba piece brilliantly captured the young, bitter, and surprisingly well-educated draftee riflemen of 1969. A platoon leader in the 101st Airborne: "Out of 28 guys, I have six college graduates, one with a masters . . . 10 guys with some college and all but one with high school diplomas. All but four of them were drafted. . . . All of them hate this war."[2]

CHAPTER 3

This was Richard Nixon's army, an army on its way home, but only gradually, only in piecemeal fashion. It was an army disintegrating from within. Whatever élan attached to the first years of military buildup, the Marines in Đà Nẵng, the 1st Cavalry in the Ia Drang, was dead. "All the early romance and idealism were gone," Sterba wrote. "Their flickering lights were snuffed on June 8, when President Nixon announced withdrawal in a statement... that must stick in the minds of every mother and father whose son has since left home for his year of war." America was getting out, and no one wanted to be the last American to die for what Nixon had concluded was a mistake. The war would be won or lost by "Asian boys," as Lyndon Johnson had once falsely averred. And so the troops drew peace signs on their helmets, wore peace symbols and love beads. "From 100 yards away, they looked like soldiers," Sterba wrote. "From ten feet away, they almost looked like a tribe of flower children with frags." And so the throwing of flowers and leaves, noted by Rogers, became a kind of hippie benediction.[3]

This was David Rogers's experience, one he would later consider "corrupting." Born in 1946 in Middletown, New Jersey, into an Irish Catholic family—his father a research chemist at Merck. He was educated in the local public schools, later at a private school in Elizabeth, New Jersey, where he never felt quite at home, and then later at Hamilton College, a well-respected liberal arts college in Upstate New York. He majored in English and history, served as the managing editor of the college newspaper—an intimation of his future—read Russian history, along with Orwell, Hemingway, Dickens, a conventional curriculum and a career path often leading to timely job offers—if it had only been a few years earlier.[4]

This was instead the mid-to-late '60s, and hard, life-altering decisions were necessary. Rogers was not an activist. He recalled joining only one demonstration, though likely only to accompany a friend. During his sophomore year, he considered enlisting in the navy but backed away. In a self-deprecating comment, he admitted to not being "very bright about it all." I'm not sure we should take him at his word. He is self-deprecating to a fault, a serious man uncomfortable exhibiting gravitas. This would become clear in an interview on C-Span in 1994 near to the height of his journalistic success at *The Wall Street Journal*, when he would refer to himself as just an "aging hack."[5]

A photograph had inspired his decision. He had come to be opposed to the war, and more than that, opposed to killing. Dorothy Day was an inspiration. He admired the Berrigans. The photograph he recalled was of a navy corpsman in Hué—Tet '68—holding a bottle of Ringer's lactate after inserting an IV into the arm of a wounded Marine. "I could do that," Rogers told me. And so he applied to his draft board in Red Bank, New Jersey, as a CO willing to serve as a medic. "My father had become a Quaker," he wrote in an email, "and was furious when I agreed to go as IAO [the Selective Service System's designation for a conscientious objector willing to serve in the army] . . . but it was '68 and I felt someone else down the street would go in my place." He would come to reconsider his father's advice. His draft board accepted his claim as a Roman Catholic pacifist.[6]

"I felt someone else down the street would go in my place." This was an uncommon attitude, and to give voice to it is a measure of Rogers's sense of citizenship and neighborly compassion. It is an attitude utterly foreign to all those who gamed the draft as two of our recent presidents, and countless others, did. But it's also foreign to those of us—I include myself—who sought only to protect their own moral honor. I cannot recall ever thinking, in all my moral struggles in those years, that my willingness to serve as a CO medic meant that someone else would not have to serve.

When I met David Rogers in the summer of 2017, in the house in Takoma Park, Maryland, he shared with his wife Rebecca, I knew that he suffered from late-onset multiple sclerosis, possibly linked to Agent Orange. He had limited energy. Mornings were best, and so I came in the morning. But I had to ask him the historian's question: Was his neighborly compassion a retrospective belief? Could he be sure that he believed that then? He didn't hesitate. Yes, he believed that then.[7]

He arrived for basic training at Fort Sam Houston in August 1968. His bunkmate, Wayne Russell, was an African American Seventh-day Adventist from Los Angeles, who would later be killed in Vietnam. Rogers arrived in Vietnam in August 1969 and joined D Company, 2nd Battalion, 28th Infantry Regiment, the "Black Lions" of the 1st Infantry Division, in an area near four villages along the Saigon River, an area dominated by the Michelin rubber plantation. The worst days of the "Black Lions" were

CHAPTER 3

behind them and overall American casualty rates dropped in the second half of 1969. But this was still a dangerous place.[8]

Unlike some COs, he never carried a weapon. Unsure of how he would be treated, a training sergeant in the 1st Infantry's orientation course took him aside and told him not to worry, "that once on line and a Doc, no one would bother me." It turned out to be true, but there was a cost. To earn the respect of his fellow soldiers, he had to be willing to move under fire to treat the wounded. "The most important thing for me as a medic," he wrote, "was to move—not hunker down—and without overstating that movement was important to those around me. . . . I was an oddity for many of the men but once I showed that I would move, all that fell away."[9]

He was wounded the night of 17 November 1969, but not sufficiently to keep him from tending to more badly wounded men, one with a sucking chest wound. One man who died that night lingered long in Rogers's memory. This was Richard Hershel Green from Flushing, New York—"Richie" to one of his childhood friends. Green was 20 years old, a graduate of Queens College, married to Margie Cohen, and working for the Social Security Administration when he was drafted. "I had to go out to get him in a tough stretch of fighting in which several others were killed," Rogers wrote. "His death always haunted me because it was so very quick and he was so very new—having come only a month before."[10]

Recovering from his wound, he returned to his platoon. He was reluctant to go on R&R since it meant leaving his platoon mates ever so briefly. In late December, he "lost a boy." This was Ellis Sanford Marlin, 20 years old, from a small town in Missouri. Marlin died of multiple fragmentation wounds on 30 December 1969. His photograph on the Virtual Wall, a graduation picture perhaps, is that of a boyish young man. "[I] lost a boy," Rogers said—not a young man, not a soldier, not a comrade, the more common nouns. I've never heard the phrase before. Yet it captures both Rogers's sense of himself—a 21-year-old tending to those younger, an adult among boys, a "doc" willing to carry extra water and flares to mark a dustoff LZ (medevac landing zone), but not ammunition, as he wrote in an email, volunteering to keep the pace count to assist the platoon leader to navigate. Yet it also captures the mythos of the platoon "doc," the "mother hen" inspecting feet and insisting that his "boys" change their socks, and in the end the man willing to move under fire to try to keep them alive.[11]

Rogers finally took his R&R in Sydney hoping that it would help him forget. He returned to the 1st Infantry and earned a reprieve. In many units, medics assigned to infantry battalions rotated out of the field after six to seven months. Rogers spent time with the battalion surgeon on MEDCAP (Medical Civic Action) rounds, visits to Vietnamese villages to provide basic medical care. In the spring of 1970, the 1st Infantry went home. Rogers was reassigned to the 12th Evacuation Hospital in Củ Chi, the base camp of the 25th Infantry Division. He worked in the emergency room. Many of his "boys," with not enough time in-country, had been assigned to the 25th.[12]

He returned to New Jersey in the summer of 1970, leaving the army as an E-5, a sergeant's pay grade, and with two valor awards that he will not discuss. A friend thought he was a "basket-case." He came to respect his father's admonitions about having agreed to serve. The war had been a "corrupting experience." "Once you were in combat, rifle or not, you were part of killing," he wrote, "and it wasn't for many years that I felt I could take communion." For faithful Catholics, communion—instituted by Jesus at the Last Supper—is the heart of the Mass, a means of grace for those who have confessed their sins. David Rogers could not forgive himself.[13]

In the spring of 1971, he would travel to Washington, alone, to take part in the antiwar demonstration, which brought John Kerry to national prominence, and where veterans would return the medals they had received, many throwing them on the west lawn of the Capitol. Rogers recalled handing his medals to the then congresswoman Bella Abzug. He didn't stay long, as he had car troubles. Though he would later have contact with antiwar veterans at Harvard, he never joined Vietnam Veterans Against the War. He was not a joiner.[14]

After working for the *Perth Amboy Evening News*, where he had interned while in college, he applied and was accepted at the Harvard Design School for an MA in city planning. There he met his wife, Rebecca. But he left city planning behind to become a journalist, turning an offer from *The Boston Globe* in 1973 into a remarkable career. He first "covered Boston's neighborhoods, school desegregation and ultimately City Hall," before moving

CHAPTER 3

on to Washington in 1979 to cover Congress. He made a specialty of the mundane but important work of the House Appropriations Committee where "real things," as he sought to explain to his readers, happened: it was "how they spent your money." He cultivated a close relationship with Speaker Tip O'Neill, whom he came to respect. He reminded him of his grandfather—O'Neill "meant a lot to me." There was something "healing" in covering O'Neill and Congress after the ugliness of Boston politics in the years of school busing, O'Neill "cared a lot about people."[15]

In 1983, he moved to *The Wall Street Journal*, a decision he took after consulting with James Sterba, the reporter he had first met as a wounded medic in Vietnam. He remained with the *Journal* for 24 years, reporting on Congress, "the covert wars of the 1980s . . . the mining of Nicaraguan harbors" until 2007 when Rupert Murdoch bought the paper. He moved to *Politico* the next month. *Politico* was delighted. His new boss, who had regarded him as a mentor, wrote that "David is the best congressional reporter in the country," while citing other journalists who labeled him "the gold standard" for Hill journalists.[16]

In 2014, the Shorenstein Center on Media, Politics, and Public Policy at the Kennedy School at Harvard awarded him the David Nyhan Prize for Political Journalism; the praise for his detailed reporting was effusive. A year earlier, he had been singled out by John Kerry, who was retiring from the Senate, thanking the "reporters who catch us in the hallways, trap us, ambush us . . . working incredibly hard to get it right, people of character who cover this place as a public service, not a sport." And then directly following: "I thank David Rogers for all that he has stood for in this institution. It is hard to imagine my job without seeing him in that long green coat waiting by the elevator after a late-night vote." There was some irony in this. Rogers, like so many others including myself, had been skeptical of how a navy officer had become the leader of the Vietnam veterans' antiwar movement.[17]

Like many of us, Rogers sought to put Vietnam behind him. He knew of David Maraniss's book on the desperate battles fought by a company he later joined, but he had not read it: "Part of my denial," he said. Yet his denial was never complete. He remembered the men he knew who died, including his bunkmate in basic training, Wayne Russell. The *Globe* sent him to DC to cover the inaugural of the Vietnam Veterans Memorial—Veterans Day, 1982. He attended the reading of the names of the dead at the National Cathedral well into the morning. The piece he wrote was deeply personal and focused on the soldiers he knew—Sgt. Anthony Marian Firak, "Tony" from Chicago, 25 years old, "whose age and gentleness made him seem out of place in a guerrilla war fought more by teenagers than those over 21." "No loss so affected the soldiers who served with him," he wrote. PFC Gerald Johnson, a 20-year-old machine gunner from Edgerton, Minnesota, died in the same ambush. Ten days later it was Richard Green, whose memory so long lingered, and then in late December, the "boy," Ellis Marlin, "who went into shock and died on a helicopter" after being wounded by a mine explosion.[18]

He recalled the mood of his earlier visit to Washington to protest the war, though he did not reveal that visit to his readers, a mood marked by a "deep, almost anarchistic bitterness toward the government, and the same anger is not far below the surface now." He briefly noted the angry controversy over the Memorial's design, yet he refused to embrace it: "Many of those most critical were former officers, yet it is questionable how well they represent the dead . . . it was draftees who bore the brunt of the fighting in the later years." The "shy" Jan Scruggs, an enlisted infantryman whose idea the Memorial was, was "a more apt spokesman than Vietnam veterans have had in the past." In a later interview, he referred to the Memorial as a "well-made gravestone." He was glad that it was there. He has long come to the Wall in the early morning hours on the Sunday before Memorial Day with his two sons.[19]

Rogers's Veterans Day piece included a quote from a Marine who was at the Wall that day. Melvin Crayton thought that it was fitting that the Wall "was hidden from the casual viewer"—its back turned against Constitution Avenue. "I think we Vietnam veterans are kind of an isolated people," he said. The quote speaks to Rogers's own isolation and reticence. You had to read between the lines of his *Globe* story to understand that he had been there.[20]

Some years later, *The Wall Street Journal* would send him to Vietnam. He told me he didn't want to go back, but he did. The story he wrote from the rubber region made clear that he had been there as an infantry medic. The piece noted the region's history of French colonialism, followed by socialist collectivism, now driven by "market-oriented reforms." "To walk again in the rubber is to remember how sound carries among the trees," he wrote. "In the war it was the pop of AK-47 rifles at night. . . . Now come the footsteps of a rubber-tree tapper." The former Michelin property, now run by the "Communist-trained sons of French era rubber workers," had been replanted, extended to an area of more than 100 square miles and employing more than 10,000. Thanh An had nearly tripled in size; brick houses with indoor kitchens and plumbing marked the emergence of a new middle class. Farmers tending their own lands and making their own investment decisions have helped to diversify agriculture.[21]

In his C-SPAN interview, Rogers mentioned that he had once helped a young girl who asked him for cloth which he brought to her. When he returned, he had a picture of that young girl and was able to locate her, now a middle-aged woman whose life had improved. He told me in a later interview that he had helped her again, this time giving her $200 to dig a well. In *The Wall Street Journal* story, he writes of his meeting with Nguyen Kim Quang, the woman in question. Now 39, she works a small plot with her husband whose war wounds, serving with the VC, have weakened him. She weaves baskets to supplement her small income from the land. Her three children remain in school and last winter she bought her first television. Once living a day at a time: "Now we have savings." "But the strain on her face," Rogers wrote, "shows life is still hard." Rural Vietnam is still poor, schools are overcrowded, "chronic malnutrition" is visible in the stunted growth of children, and Rogers had doubts that the land could support a rapidly growing population.[22]

In the middle of his C-SPAN interview he gave voice to a deeper, personal frustration. "What was it all about? If all they wanted was a free market, if all they wanted was a McDonald's franchise, we could have worked this out long ago. A lot of people died for what were a set of ideas that weren't necessary." He never completed the sentence, moving on to, "I'm always struck by that memory."[23]

Memory, however intense, is not history. It's a great quote. It seems to capture the absurdity of it all, "If all they wanted was a free market." But that's not what they wanted. Lê Duẩn, Lê Đức Thọ, Hồ Chí Minh, and Võ Nguyên Giáp—the core leadership of North Vietnam—were dedicated communists, committed to a Stalinist model of economic development and the collectivization of agriculture in 1945. They would follow the same model after their 1975 victory. It did not work. In 1986, after the death of Lê Duẩn, the communist leadership announced a change of plan—Đổi Mới (renovation)—allowing for limited free market activity for farmers and small business owners. This was the new reality that Rogers reported in *The Wall Street Journal*, but it was not a truly free market. The Communist Party still controlled, and remains in control of, the major industries. David Rogers is not a student of Vietnamese history. He is a moralist, who once acted on that moralism, at the risk of his life.[24]

That moralism would come through on two more recent pieces he would write for *Politico*. The first, in July 2015, opened with "Who would have guessed it, but the Vietnam War draft could become a political issue again." In the wake of candidate Donald Trump's attack on the service of John McCain, Rogers decided to dig deeper into Trump's history with the draft. After graduating from college in 1968, after four years of student deferments, Trump received a medical deferment in the fall of that year. In the summer of 2015, Trump admitted for the first time that the deferment was for bone spurs. His campaign claimed that it was a "short-term" deferment. Trump, an athlete in his youth, claimed the bone spur was "minor," and that "I was entered into the draft and I got a very, very high draft number."[25]

Rogers saw through the story. There are no "minor" deferments, as Rogers noted. Nor are there "short-term" deferments. Eighteen months would elapse between Trump's deferment and the birthdate lottery of December 1969. Trump avoided the draft from the fall of 1968 until December 1969, the killing years for Americans in Vietnam—when the need for draftees was at its height. Trump avoided the draft because of a bone spur, a bone spur that he sought to downplay in 2015. It seemed to embarrass him. Had he brought a letter from a family doctor? "Young men with access to friendly family physicians had this advantage," Rogers wrote. "Lower income individuals, with no doctor but with health issues bigger

CHAPTER 3

than bone spurs, could find themselves approved for military service."[26]

Two weeks later, Rogers would publish a sharper critique of Trump, one that evoked his memories of the war. The occasion was the assertion by Khizr Khan, the father of a young army captain killed in Iraq, that Trump had "sacrificed nothing." Trump responded fiercely: "I have made a lot of sacrifices. I work very, very hard. . . . I've created thousands of jobs, tens of thousands. . . . I've had tremendous success. I think I've done a lot." This was not the language of sacrifice.[27]

"When Donald Trump talks about his 'sacrifices,'" Rogers wrote, "I think of Richard from Trump's own Queens." This was Richard Green, Richie to his friends, whose memory had long haunted Rogers. "Military records tell me now that Richard was 21 and would have been drafted in the same period when Trump, then 23, was enjoying a friendly medical deferment in Queens because of bone spurs." Rogers wrote, "The New York billionaire has always insisted that he was prepared to serve if he had not gotten a high lottery number in December 1969. But all the evidence shows Trump played the deferment system for better than a year until that safe number was secured."[28]

Rogers went on to acknowledge that there were "no clear-cut, moral answers for young men faced with the Vietnam draft." He had once embraced a personal "clear-cut" moral answer, but his experience had chastened him. When I challenged him in an interview that his willingness to serve as a CO medic was that answer, he would have none of it. If I had served as a line medic in an infantry battalion instead of in a medical company in a protected base camp, he told me, I might think differently. He could well be right. So we have to leave it at that—no "clear-cut" moral answers.[29]

He had more to say, however—a direct challenge to Donald Trump and all those who gamed the draft. Immediately following the no "clear-cut" moral answers sentence was this: "One thing was certain. If you didn't go, someone else like a Richard would effectively take your place." That was the heart of his decision to serve as a CO medic, however tainted he later felt. "If I didn't go someone else would have to go in my place."[30]

CHAPTER 4

Five Adventists from the Mid-Atlantic

Seventh-day Adventists made up roughly half of all conscientious objector medics, yet their stories remain largely untold. As we've seen earlier, the church had a long tradition of encouraging its young men to serve but not to kill. Church leaders, voicing their patriotism, saw themselves as "conscientious cooperators" rather than "objectors." The stories of the young Adventists who served as medics in Vietnam deserve their hearing both in this chapter and in later chapters.[1]

Tom Hirst and Nolan Byrd were high school friends; Hirst, Jay Diller, and Terry Sewell knew each other in school and college; and Byrd and William Hall knew each other in basic training. Four went to war; two of those came home. They shared a faith, at least for a time. They were Seventh-day Adventists (SDAs) all from the mid-Atlantic. Four of them, following the strictures of their church, would serve as conscientious objector (CO) medics. "All us guys knew we might eventually be called upon to fulfill our military obligation," Tom Hirst wrote, "in a noncombatant position."[2]

The term "noncombatant" obscures the truth. Some medics served in hospitals and aid stations, but the overwhelming majority, especially in the years of intensive combat from 1967 to 1969, served in infantry companies and knew what it meant to be under fire, knew what it meant to try to save a life, and even knew what it meant to be a combatant.

Tom Hirst and Nolan Byrd came to know all that. They were childhood friends and for a time lived near each other—the Byrds in Langley

CHAPTER 4

Park, Maryland, the Hirsts in nearby Silver Spring. They spent Saturday afternoons together after church: "wrestling was a favorite hobby" of both Nolan and his brother Byron. "I used to wrestle both of them at the same time," Hirst recalled. "Nolan was also a pretty good athlete and was a very fast runner. . . . Byron was more of a 'ladies man.'"[3]

The Byrd family had roots near Hagerstown, Maryland. Nolan's father owned an autobody shop near there, and he and Tom Hirst's father, an insurance adjuster, had business dealings with each other. The area was also home to Mt. Aetna Camp, an Adventist campground hosting the Pathfinders, the Adventist version of the Scouts. Tom Hirst recalled the shared campouts. At some point prior to 1965, the Byrds left Langley Park for Hagerstown and Tom and Nolan drifted apart.[4]

The Hirsts stayed in Silver Spring. Both of Tom's parents were active in the Adventist church. His mother worked in the mailroom of the General Conference of the church—its then world headquarters—in nearby Takoma Park (it is now in Silver Spring). He graduated from Takoma Academy in 1967. He looks serious in his class picture, wearing a bowtie with horn-rimmed glasses, his gravity underscored by his full name: Thomas Edward Hirst.[5]

The serious pose belied a very different spirit. His picture is captioned: "He is the picture of content as he zooms to work or school on his motorcycle. To be exact, he always looks contented. He takes the best of things out of life and ignores the rest. Food, football, baseball, basketball and co-education are the finer things in Tom's life." Tom was known by one of his peers as only loosely attached to Adventist principles. His second-grade teacher, in a report card, had labeled him "irreverent."[6]

One of Tom's classmates at Takoma Academy was Terry Sewell, born in Baltimore, who was two years behind him. Terry's grandfather and mother were active in the First Adventist Church where he was dedicated and confirmed. He went to public school through eighth grade, then to Atholton Junior Academy in Columbia, Maryland, an Adventist school, for ninth grade, and then in the fall of 1966 to Blue Mountain Academy in Hamburg, Pennsylvania, an Adventist boarding school for one semester only. He would finish his high school education at Takoma Academy.[7]

While at Blue Mountain, Terry came to know Jay Thomas Diller. Diller, born in 1948, was from Chambersburg, Pennsylvania. The two served a suspension together working on a new gym being built. Jay had gone to a dance in Hershey without permission; Terry had ventured off campus to New Jersey. Terry remembered Jay as a bouncy, energetic young man without meanness, deviousness, or pretense. He appears earnest, staring straight at the camera, handsome, clean-cut in jacket and tie with the merest hint of a smile in his class photo. Another photo captured him in a candid moment enjoying ice cream with his then girlfriend Nancy May. Blue Mountain encouraged its graduates to indicate their proposed college major. J. Thomas Diller, as he styled himself, intended to study business administration. Diller would go on to Columbia Union College, another Adventist school, in Silver Spring.[8]

So too would Tom Hirst. "I did what my parents wanted me to do," he wrote, "stay in school." He knew Diller, but not well. Hirst was a "townie," Diller lived in the dorms. Hirst knew Diller as Tom and remembered him as good-looking with a clean-cut "preppie" look. Diller had a new girlfriend, the athletic Laura Benn. They were engaged.[9]

Hirst did not last long at Columbia Union. After a year, he dropped out. It was the spring of 1968. He would later write that he was "just getting tired of the religious aspect of everything." He went to work for a Dodge dealer in Washington, DC: "My life was work and fast cars, a girlfriend and spending most every weekend at the local drag strips. Life was good!"[10]

Meanwhile, his high school friend Nolan Byrd had been drafted, reporting to basic training at Fort Sam Houston, to the Long Barracks, in May 1968. The Long Barracks, built in the late nineteenth century, had been the home of CO basic since 1954, an abbreviated six-week stint—all but the rifle range—meant to instill military discipline, to strengthen shoulders, legs, and overall conditioning, indispensable strengths for those likely to serve in the infantry.[11]

At Fort Sam Houston, Byrd met William Hall. They were in the same basic training class. Hall was an African American from Philadelphia; Byrd was white and his home of record was in Hagerstown, in Western Maryland. They went to church together, their Adventist faith more important than

CHAPTER 4

their racial differences. Graduating from basic, they moved across post to begin ten weeks of medical training—a mix of field first aid, administering shots, and making beds with "hospital corners." In the fall of 1968, according to Hall, every medical graduate had orders for Vietnam.[12]

William Hall, born in 1948, grew up in an Adventist family. His brother John was also a CO medic who served in Vietnam and who had returned home prior to the fall of 1968. His brother-in-law had been a Whitecoat, a CO medic who had volunteered for medical experimentation, a program open only to Adventist COs. Not every basic training class had the opportunity to so volunteer. Hall's class had not had the opportunity, but he told me he wouldn't have volunteered: "I never wanted to be a test tube."[13]

Hall's first assignment was to the MACV (Military Assistance Command, Vietnam) headquarters dispensary in Saigon. He worked there until January 1968 when he was reassigned to the 11th Armored Cavalry Regiment. He learned from a friend, Joe Butler from Baltimore, that he would be replacing Nolan Byrd, who had died in combat. Tom Hirst had heard the news a month earlier.[14]

Byrd had arrived in-country on 23 October 1968. He was assigned to Headquarters and Headquarters Troop, 2nd Squadron, 11th Armored Cavalry Regiment. He was 20 years old, a Private First Class (PFC). Seven weeks later he was dead. Hall had been told he died from a direct hit on a bunker. The official record was less precise—cause of death was "artillery, rocket, or mortar fire," in Bình Dương Province. He "died outright," his body recovered. His was the only death that day. Years later both Hall and Hirst would post remembrances on the "Wall of Faces" website, where a smiling Nolan Byrd, his head canted to the left, continues to stare out at us. He is buried at Gettysburg National Cemetery.[15]

Hall served with the 11th Armored Cavalry for a full year in the field. He had extended to complete his two years. Like some COs, he chose to carry an M16. Wounded twice, he was promoted to squadron medic and left the army as a Specialist 5th Class, with the pay grade of a sergeant. The war, he told me, was a "horrible experience" and he did not want to talk further about it. When he returned he wanted to connect with Byrd's family and so contacted Byrd's pastor. Hall's memory was that the pastor was no help, and simply "wanted to get off the phone." He never did connect with the family.¹⁶

Meanwhile, in the summer of 1969, Terry Sewell was planning his future, Tom Hirst was awaiting a draft notice, and Jay Diller, whatever his college plans had been, would soon report to Fort Sam Houston for basic training. Sewell graduated from Takoma Academy in 1969. He had been class treasurer: "fast cars, food, cycling, the opposite sex" were among his favorites, noted below his class picture.¹⁷

Opposition to the war was building. Young Adventists had begun to question why they should serve as CO medics. Sewell too turned against the war in the early 1970s—it seemed to him that the US was "not trying to win." During the summer of 1969, he suffered a serious accident while working. A fall from a roof led to a concussion and broken wrist bones. Not sure that the accident would disqualify him from service, he learned in December 1969 that his draft lottery number was in the single digits. On a holiday trip to Florida with a friend from Takoma Academy and his family, he met a businessman who worked in Canada. When he was offered a job, he considered a move to Canada. He never had to act on the offer. His injuries were sufficient for him to fail the army physical. He would serve out the remainder of the war years as a student at the University of Georgia where he earned a degree in veterinary medicine.¹⁸

Tom Hirst received his draft notice in August 1969. He would be inducted in October and began basic training shortly after. While in basic, he had the opportunity to volunteer for the Whitecoat program. Not every Adventist recruit did. A team of evaluators, made up of Army Medical Corps officers and elders of the SDA church, would come to San Antonio just twice a year. When the program was first instituted after the Korean War, it had only a limited appeal. Those who were chosen were promised a two-year tour in the Washington DC/Frederick, Maryland, area, near the world headquarters of the church. Those who chose not to volunteer, for whatever reason, could end up serving in the peacetime army in the US, Germany, or Korea. By 1965, all that changed. Selection for the Whitecoat program was a ticket out of the Vietnam War. In the years of war, an overwhelming majority of Adventists who had the opportunity to volunteer did

CHAPTER 4

so. One young Adventist, who made it his goal to know when the interviews would take place, actually timed his induction to ensure that his training would coincide with the visit of army officers and church elders. The presence of the elders offered the potential for favoritism, even nepotism, though Hirst told me had no proof of it. Tom Hirst wasn't selected for the Whitecoat program that fall. One of the elders was someone who knew him, or knew of him, and knew his mother who worked at the church's headquarters. Years later, Hirst came to believe that his early reputation as "irreverent" had caught up to him. More than that, the elder's daughter, according to Hirst, enjoyed riding on Hirst's motorcycle.[19]

After completing basic and the standard ten weeks of medical training, Hirst had his orders in late December for Vietnam, along with all those whose last names began with A and ran through M. The rest of the alphabet went to Germany. Granted a 45-day leave, he would arrive in Vietnam on 5 March 1970. The army assigned him to the 12th Cavalry Regiment, 1st Cavalry Division at Sông Bé. For a week he worked in the base camp aid station and then learned he was to join 3rd Platoon, Charlie Company, 1st Battalion of the 12th Infantry. He recalled that he was offered a .45 pistol, a weapon that medics were authorized to carry. This was a defining moment for him and for many other COs. Hirst declined the .45 and chose to carry an M16. Years later, he would write that the M16 was a much better "patient protector"—"reality is what it is."[20]

He spent a day at LZ Snuffy and then boarded a helicopter for the field. Charlie Company was in contact with one dead and one wounded. "When the chopper landed, I jumped off as a 'body bag' was loaded on. One hell of a way to spend Easter Sunday." He made a point of remembering that a soldier named Ken Garski was in that body bag.[21]

For the next seven and one-half months, Hirst spent his time "humping the jungles" with 75 pounds on his back. He was relatively lucky. He treated minor injuries, including jungle rot, while overseeing the army's malaria protocols. His company had to report to battalion every morning that all the troops had been seen taking their daily pills. The first time he had to medevac a platoon member, Greg Egan, it was the result of an allergic reaction to a bee sting.[22]

All this would change on 29 April, when Charlie Company's commander, Cpt. Michael Christy, got a call ordering him back to Fire Support Base Buttons. The next day he learned that the entire battalion would be airlifted into Cambodia "to find and destroy NVA [North Vietnamese Army] sanctuaries." Enemy resistance was likely to be strong and heavy casualties were to be expected. The order would soon filter down to Hirst and his fellow soldiers. They would draw new equipment, "weapons were recalibrated and test fired. Medics swapped out their medical bag contents for fresh supplies." Hirst remembered the presence of new replacements and of weapons not usually carried—M-72 LAWs (Light Anti-Tank Weapon), and 90mm recoilless rifles.[23]

Charlie Company had to wait a day before there were enough helicopters available. On 2 May, twenty helicopters airlifted the company to a landing zone five kilometers across the border. Within an hour they spotted their first five NVAs. Hoping to lure them closer, Christy ordered his men to hold fire, but one soldier failed to heed the order, and the NVAs escaped. At 1630, Charlie established a night defensive position in a grove of trees, but not before setting up Claymores and grenades linked to a tripwire on a likely trail. Just before dawn, the automatic ambush claimed the life of an NVA soldier on his bicycle, his transistor radio on.[24]

A few days later, as Charlie Company was awaiting resupply, 2nd Platoon came across a "huge truck park and maintenance shop." There were thirty-three vehicles, most of them Ford trucks, along with a large parts department with "welding tools, barrels of gasoline and cases of oil." The complex included underground sleeping quarters, a mess hall, an aid station, and fifty tons of rice. Battalion ordered all serviceable vehicles to Fire Support Base Evans.[25]

Tom Hirst was in his métier. It felt like being "home again," back in that Dodge dealership in DC, this time with American jeeps and Land Rovers. Hirst began tinkering and was able to hotwire many of the vehicles. Christy sent ten back-loaded with captured supplies, but kept two to carry the men's packs, "making Charlie Company a kind of quasi-mechanized unit," as Hirst remembered: "It only lasted a couple of days until we got back into thicker jungle but those two days were like heaven."[26]

CHAPTER 4

The company blew up and burned what was left of the NVA motor pool and set in for the night. Third platoon saw flashlights and heard Vietnamese voices moving toward them. Christy had set out Claymores and grenades and they did their work. Hirst recalls his platoon firing and throwing grenades, though Christy did not mention that. Both heard the agonized death throes of an NVA soldier: "moaning, groaning, and dying out there. It was pretty crazy," as Hirst recalled. This was his first exposure to combat and to the deafening noise of small arms fire—you "wanted to put fingers in your ears," he said. Later that night, they heard a single shot.[27]

At first light, they discovered nine dead, one an apparent suicide. They also found a wounded NVA soldier whom they evacuated using the jungle penetrator attached to the medevac helicopter. Hirst recalled the extraction as ungraceful, with the wounded soldier bouncing off several trees as he was hoisted up. He later learned that he had died.[28]

Forty days in, Christy recalled a highly successful mission, twenty-five enemy soldiers killed, caches of food and weapons and an entire motor pool destroyed. Far better, Charlie had suffered no deaths. All this would change on 14 June. In search of a bunker complex, Charlie's 1st Platoon walked into an NVA ambush. Hirst recalled that his 3rd Platoon had been in drag, the infantry term used for those holding down the rear of the formation. Christy repositioned them on the enemy's left flank.[29]

The company remained out of radio contact until Christy found shelter behind a tree and ordered his radio telephone operator Specialist Tom Thon to place his radio as high above his head as possible. Thon wasn't pleased, but he did it and it worked. Artillery support and gunships were on their way.[30]

Meanwhile, 1st Platoon took casualties. Sgt. Mickey Wright died while charging a bunker; the point man, Specialist Tom Johnson, known as "the Black Prince," was hit. Treated quickly by medic Larry Stansberry and pulled to safety by his fellow platoon members, Johnson survived, lifted out with a jungle penetrator after the artillery and gunships had done their work. The jungle fell silent, as Charlie moved toward the badly damaged bunker surrounded by trees that had been "ripped apart." Charlie found blood trails, but no casualties, though a day later they would find ten fresh graves.[31]

On 28 June, Christy received orders to move his company back to Vietnam. They were to be the last company out. Journalists and TV reporters descended. The trek back turned hard. A muddy log across a river provided a bridge and they would settle in for the night near Fire Support Base Thor in quarters so tight that it concerned Christy.[32]

He was right to be concerned. Around 0500, two mortar rounds landed among his sleeping troops. Friendly fire. "Wounded men were screaming in pain," Christy wrote, "others were screaming for medics." The company medic, Bruce Johnson, was among those badly hit. Christy radioed the firebase for more medics and called in a medevac. His next story falls outside the standard tale of heroic medevac pilots. The pilot, thinking the attack had come from the enemy, refused to land without gunship support—standard protocol though not always observed. Christy explained it was friendly fire, begged, and then grew irate. "Look, I have your tail number. I know who you are and if you don't start down immediately, I swear to God, I will find you and put a bullet in your brain." The pilot requested a flare and landed. Two men died and 29 were wounded, seriously enough to be evacuated from Vietnam. Christy later learned the mortar rounds had behaved erratically, but they "should never have been fired over our position."[33]

Hirst remembered the chaos of that night, bandaging a soldier whose right triceps had been blown off, inserting an IV for Ringer's lactate, a blood expander, and using two morphine syrettes to dull the soldier's pain while waiting for the delayed medevac. Hirst himself had been wounded— shrapnel in his shoulder and backside—although he didn't realize it at the time. Less forgiving than Christy, he claimed that the friendly fire incident had been "swept under the rug." He could find no record of it in a later search in the National Archives. A full forty years later, he and other survivors were still "trying to come to grips with that tragic incident. Hirst was awarded the Army Commendation Medal with V clip, denoting valor, for his actions that night."[34]

Jay Thomas Diller arrived in Vietnam on the third of January 1970. He had left Columbia Union sometime earlier, losing his student deferment. He would have completed basic training and medical training by the late fall of 1969. Once in-country, he was assigned to Headquarters and

CHAPTER 4

Headquarters Company, 2nd Battalion, 501st Infantry, 101st Airborne Division. On the fifth of May he was at Fire Support Base Henderson in Quảng Trị Province. He arrived late that afternoon, a member of 1st Lt. Richard A. Hawley's recon platoon, serving as reinforcements for Alpha Company.[35]

Alpha Company was understrength and had been taking casualties since the middle of April. "Hard-luck Alpha," as it was known, had also lost experienced soldiers as the result of army policy. Reenlistment sergeants were only too happy to offer young soldiers a transfer to the rear if they were willing to re-up for an additional year or more, and transfer they did. Alpha Company left an embattled hill position, known as "Re-Up Hill." They would take further casualties, seven KIA (Killed in Action) and seven wounded, while defending Fire Support Base (FSB) Granite from a sapper attack on 29 April.[36]

On the morning of May 5, Alpha had orders to secure FSB Henderson in what was considered to be a relatively quiet area, in order to regroup and await reinforcements from Hawley's recon platoon. It did not go well. According to Keith Nolan: "It took the company all day to establish its positions and set up Claymores. There was no time to make use of the concertina wire that had been flown in, or to clear fields with fire. . . . No security patrols were run, no listening posts deployed."[37]

Whatever Alpha Company's faults, FSB Henderson had further problems. Ammunition was lying in the open on pallets, including a thousand rounds of 155mm artillery shells. They had not been covered or revetted (enclosed behind sandbags) despite instructions to do so by the brigade commander Col. William Bradley.[38]

Sappers attacked on the morning of the sixth, supported by NVA assault troops. Satchel charges, or a Soviet-made flamethrower, detonated the ammo dump, "showering us with shrapnel," according to one eyewitness account. The explosion devastated the recon platoon, killing most of them including the platoon leader. George Banda recalled seeing Doc Diller "lying there on his back as if he were asleep. I tried to pick him up and saw the back of [Diller's] head was gone." Jay Thomas Diller was one of twenty-five Americans killed that morning. Maj. Robert Turner, the battalion operations officer, claimed that Colonel Bradley was livid because if they had revetted the ammo as instructed, one satchel charge wouldn't have ended up destroying most of the firebase.[39]

Ray Wenger, his cousin, wrote: "I'll never forget the day the Red Cross summoned me from field duty; I knew the news was not going to be good but I never thought it would be about Tommy." Diller's parents had asked Wenger to accompany his body home. "Tommy and I played together as kids. One of many lasting memories were the unusual sandwiches he taught me.... Bread, peanut butter, slice of onion and ketchup. He saw me give my first kiss to a girl on a swing near his home.... So it was a long trip home to meet the body at Dover... and make the flight to Hagerstown, and prepare mentally for his funeral." Jay Thomas Diller is buried at Norland Cemetery, Chambersburg, Pennsylvania.[40]

After the War

Tom Hirst applied his mechanical skills to the repair of boats and worked for a time for Zodiac of North America where his team developed a prototype of the F470 Assault boat still in use by the military. He moved to Florida in 1984 and returned to the civilian boating business, running the parts department at a Cummins dealership in St. Petersburg.[41]

William Hall became an Adventist pastor. most recently serving a church in Willow Grove, Pennsylvania. The Reverend William E. Hall Sr. died in August 2024.[42]

Terry Sewell and his wife Karen built a large veterinary practice in Buckeystown, Maryland. We met on a tour of Martin Luther sites in Germany commemorating the 500th anniversary of the Reformation. An awkward conversation at a restaurant in Wittenberg led to an emotional moment for him as he recalled the life of Tom Diller. He and his wife later welcomed me to their home where this story I've recounted had its origin. Terry died young, in March 2020. Karen continues to preside over Buckeystown Veterinary Hospital.[43]

CHAPTER 5

A Death in Khe Sanh

It was possible to claim to be a conscientious objector even after enlisting. Jonathan Spicer, a young, naive, and deeply religious Marine was one who did so. The normal path for such a claim led through a chaplain, who would attest to the sincerity of the claim, and then to higher headquarters for a final decision. A positive decision typically led to separation from the military. Spicer's claim, affirmed by a chaplain, never reached higher headquarters. Offered a position as a stretcher-bearer, he remained at Khe Sanh during the siege forever associated with that place. Jonathan Spicer would die there, awarded a Navy Cross for his heroism, unrecognized as a conscientious objector.

Jonathan Spicer left no public account of his life. We know him only through the accounts of others. He joined the Marines, according to his father, a former Methodist pastor, "only because he thought he could get into the K-9 division, but it didn't work out that way.... Jonathan's great love was horses and dogs." He was "a gentle boy" who "reads the Bible every day." "The last I heard," his father said, "he was halfway through the Book of Leviticus."[1]

The Marines made him an infantryman and assigned him to Khe Sanh prior to the prolonged siege of 1968. Ray Stubbe, a Lutheran pastor and one of Khe Sanh's chaplains, met him there on 12 January 1968, before the start of the siege. Spicer had just arrived. "He came in—a very 'boyish' kind of appearance, demeanor," Stubbe recalled, "he looked like he was 12, 13

CHAPTER 5

years old." He told Stubbe that he was a conscientious objector, that his hero was Albert Schweitzer. "He told me—I'll never forget; some of these things are engraved in my memory—he said: He didn't care what happened to him; he just didn't want to hurt anyone else." Stubbe noted this in a diary entry for that day: "He said he's not afraid to give up his life and would like to work for the people here. He just doesn't want to kill. We immediately began the paperwork to write up his application."[2]

Spicer told Stubbe that his recruiters said he could be a dog handler and that he wouldn't have to go into combat. "Well, the recruiters in those days—we know—would do anything to get their quota." Spicer had first claimed conscientious objector status in boot camp, later at Camp Pendleton awaiting assignment to Vietnam. They kept telling him wait until you get to your next duty station, Stubbe recalled, "they just didn't want to handle it, or they thought that maybe he'd crack and conform."[3]

Pvt. George Anderson recalled Spicer's arrival in Khe Sanh. "Everything was going real good, when the Sgt. told me that one of the guys wouldn't take his weapon. It turned out to be Spicer. Let's face it, we really got on that kid. But he held on to that big old Bible and kept saying that no matter what we did to him he still loved us. That kinda pissed me off.... I thought he was a coward." A second Marine, Cpl. Earl K. Clark, recalled his perplexed and frustrated company commander questioning "how in the world [Spicer] managed to get into a combat infantry unit if he was a bona fide conscientious objector." Clark also recalled Spicer's "sincerity and honesty: 'I believe in my heart that PFC Spicer was a CO.'"[4]

So too did Ray Stubbe. Stubbe was a young man, 29 years old. He had been ordained little more than two years earlier, after serving two years as a seaman in the Naval Reserve, later graduating from St. Olaf's College in philosophy, and then graduating second in his class from seminary. He was a scholar, trained in Greek and Hebrew, and had been accepted into a PhD program at the University of Chicago. A long career as a seminary professor beckoned. He chose instead to be a Navy chaplain and arrived in Khe Sanh, as a chaplain to Marines, in 1967. Spicer was not the first Marine to come to him with a conscientious objector claim. He recalled at least one officer with such a claim.[5]

An interview with the chaplain was only the first step in an administrative process that was overseen by the Pentagon. The chaplain had the duty to attest to the religious sincerity of the applicant, following a rigorous and detailed format dictated by the military entailing such questions as under what circumstances the applicant would use force, but he had no authority to decide the case. "The Department of Defense made it very difficult for conscientious objectors" claiming such status after enlistment. According to Stubbe: "They had a long hard process almost Herculean in scope."[6]

Stubbe said he kept a file of "all" those who came to him. "I was very liberal," he said, "with a sort of enlightened self-preservation." If men didn't want to fire their weapons, they were a danger to other Marines and to Stubbe himself, he remembered, as he sometimes shared isolated outposts with his fellow Marines: "My feeling was that if a fellow came in and said that he had any doubts at all if he would fire on the enemy, then that person should not be in that situation." "So my feeling," he went on, "was 'get rid of them' . . . so I was very supportive of all conscientious objectors." Spicer's was the only name he recalled, and the only one he singled out as "a very genuine conscientious objector." The "other people I supported, I supported; I just didn't know."[7]

Stubbe told Spicer he would start the process: "We'll write this up and we'll take care of it." In the meantime, Spicer had to go back to his supply unit. In the normal course, Spicer, like the other prospective conscientious objectors who came to Stubbe, would have to wait for orders bringing him and the others back to divisional headquarters where they could reasonably expect to be assigned to fatigue details while Marine bureaucracy began a process that would not end until it reached Washington.[8]

Then the siege started. A day or so after, Spicer's first sergeant came to Stubbe. "Chaplain . . . you have to do something about Spicer. . . . He won't take up his rifle and clean it and the guys are beating him up." Stubbe recalled: "I can understand that. When things get tense, people—especially the Marines—they have to depend on each other, and if there's a 'weak link'—it's just like a hen pecking, the birds pecking the weak bird."[9]

Stubbe offered a solution. Stubbe had an opening for a chaplain's clerk, a position he didn't really need. Stubbe's bunker was in the medical company

CHAPTER 5

area. So he told the first sergeant, "assign him to me, and he'll work for 3rd Platoon, Charlie Company 'Charlie Med' . . . He can be a stretcher-bearer. . . . So he reported to me. And I have to say to my shame, again, that was the last time I saw him, because I was all over the base all the time, and I didn't want him around me. I didn't want to be responsible for protecting him. . . . And I didn't pursue any more of his conscientious objection thing."[10]

Stubbe, who became the unofficial historian of the siege of Khe Sanh and the keeper of its memories, carried for years a deep guilt over Spicer's death. "For the longest time I had guilt feelings," he told me. Once the siege started, however, there was little chance that he could complete the paperwork necessary to Spicer's conscientious objector application. "There was no more paperwork," he told me, after the siege started. Yet he still felt guilt. If he hadn't intervened Spicer might have been beaten up by his peers, or possibly disciplined, but he still would have been alive. At some point, a fellow veteran consoled him: Spicer "was just doing what he had to do, and you were doing what you had to do. It just happened."[11]

In a recent phone conversation, Reverend Stubbe gave voice to the deepest stirrings of Lutheran theology. We live in a sinful world—a broken world—and all of us are broken and none of our actions are free of sin. Stubbe believed that war brought out the harshest meanings of moral choice. He mentioned decisions that his commander had made, one involving Laotian refugees, another involving a Special Forces camp. In war, there are no easy, morally clear choices. Those thoughts had helped to console him.[12]

Stubbe recalled that Spicer led the working parties that carried the wounded on stretchers to the waiting helicopters. This was a dangerous job. As the siege wore on, NVA artillery had zeroed in the landing zone. Stubbe witnessed Spicer staying with the wounded, at times lying down on top of them: "He'd lay down beside the stretcher and try to comfort the guy or even lay on top of him to give him more assurance."[13] Dan Sullivan, an ambulance driver for Charlie Med: "I saw him put his life on the line, picking up wounded Marines . . . while dodging incoming."

Lt. James Finnigan, one of the Navy doctors serving in Charlie Med, recalled Spicer: "The kid was not a coward. He just didn't want to be a shooter. So he became our main litter-bearer. He would run back and forth to the choppers under fire. The kid was fearless. We loved him."[14]

Finnigan remembered the day Spicer was hit, as he and his fellow doctors were standing down: "Suddenly somebody yelled, 'Spicer's down!' He was moving litters and took shrapnel right though the center of his chest." Finnigan continues the story: "They brought him quickly into triage, right onto the first litter. He was gone. No pulse. No blood pressure. Don Magilligan was standing beside me and said, 'I think it's pericardial tamponade.'" The blood in the heart sac was compressing the heart, the result of a fragment piercing the heart through the pericardium. The hole was small enough so that blood spurted out of the heart into the sac. Finnigan thought Magilligan was right. "So we opened his chest, massaged his heart, put a single stitch in his heart, and his vital signs came back. Everything seemed dandy." He had been stabilized. That was all Charlie Med could do. That was their job. Spicer was medevacked to Đà Nẵng.[15]

Once a patient is medevacked, it's common that doctors and medics lose track of that patient. That happened with Spicer. Finnigan: "For a long time nobody could find out what happened to him." They finally learned that after being medevacked from Đà Nẵng to Japan, he died of infection. "It's hard to know," Finnigan recalled, "exactly what that means." The initial story of Charlie Med's deft intervention was widely reported. "We were very excited because we thought we had saved our boy."[16]

John Randolph, a journalist present in Khe Sanh, wrote the story, burying the lede in the third paragraph. Spicer's pacifism, which Randolph never acknowledged, would take second place to a story about jungle boots. *The Los Angeles Times*'s editors would make it worse, writing a headline, "Those Jungle Boots Echo from Khe Sanh," an incoherent and tone-deaf lede.[17]

The boots in question belonged to a brave and intrepid woman journalist, Jurate Kazickas. A freelancer, she had arrived in Khe Sanh on the 7th of March. Much to the disgust of the Marines' public information officer, she had jumped the queue. The Marines limited the number of journalists allowed at Khe Sanh and managed a queue attempting to be fair to newspapers and wire services all wanting a story. Kazickas, a slim and attractive 24-year-old, six feet tall with flowing hair, had little

CHAPTER 5

difficulty, as she later admitted, in cadging rides with accommodating helicopter pilots.[18]

The next day, fragments from an NVA mortar shell struck Kazickas, wounding her in her forearm, lower leg, and buttocks while also stippling her face with metal, dirt, and pebbles. "I've been hit. . . . I've been hit," she said while her tape recorder ran. Years later, she would sometimes replay the tape. Marines brought her to the aid station where as a wounded woman her presence would alter established protocols. Randolph reported that Finnigan and the other doctors "chased away all eager volunteers." Years later, Kazickas recalled that the doctors "ordered the corpsmen to hang up some blankets to give me a modicum of privacy" and decided not to scissor off her fatigues which was standard practice but to ask where she thought she had been hit. Someone saw blood on the seat of her pants, so she rolled over and pulled them down. "Is it below my bikini line?" she joked. Told it was, she continued to use earthy banter to deflect her embarrassment. "Tell me, honestly, does my bottom look that different from the hundreds of others you've seen in here? . . . In spite of myself, I was miffed when he replied, 'Well, to be honest, not really.'"[19]

Corpsmen, Spicer included, would soon rush her on a stretcher to a waiting helicopter on her way to Đông Hà and then to the hospital in Đà Nẵng. She left behind a pair of discarded jungle boots, size 9. According to the story first told by Randolph, Spicer, "a real half-pint," was in need of boots that fit for he was "wearing the sleazy black high-topped sneakers issued to Vietnamese soldiers." Kazickas's boots were now Spicer's. Spicer was pleased. Randolph reported his last sighting of Spicer condescendingly: "I watched the funny, happy, little marine hopping about, warming us all with his own joy."[20]

There is much about the boots story that seems improbable. The Marine Corps is full of short men, and size nine boots are not an especially small size. Whatever the problems of resupply at Khe Sanh, and they were many, it's hard to believe that Spicer would not have been fitted with size nine boots prior to deployment. Perhaps he lost or misplaced them once in Vietnam. In any case, Randolph and at least one of the doctors would attest to the story and it would be retold years later by Kazickas, who never knew him, a bathetic note to a much larger story of conscience and valor.

The Navy awarded Spicer the Navy Cross, its second highest award for valor. Private Spicer "unhesitatingly volunteered to serve as a stretcher-bearer . . . disregarding his own safety, he continued to expedite the loading of the wounded . . . despite the increasing intensity of the attack, and was the last man to seek shelter." He left the safety of his own position to assist the exposed wounded. He was hit while he "shielded a Marine from the blast with his own body." Unable to walk, "he warned his comrades to remain in their protective positions while he attempted to crawl" to safety. "His selfless actions undoubtedly prevented serious injury or possible death to his fellow Marines and were an inspiration to all who observed them." The citation never mentioned that he had applied for conscientious objector status and had refused to carry a weapon.[21]

His "selfless actions" deserve to be remembered and honored. But how do we explain such "selfless actions"? The reasons, the beliefs, or the instincts that led Jonathan Nathaniel Spicer to abjure killing and to do what he did to protect the lives of the vulnerable have died with him. The standard answer from countless men awarded valor medals is "I was just doing my job." Just doing my job. A Marine corpsman's job is to answer the call "corpsman up." And so most did. And so did I once, answering the army call "medic." I recall hesitating, ever so briefly, but I was the medic and this was my job. And so I rose up from my protected position and moved forward, truth be told, to avoid embarrassment and the contempt of my peers. It was my job. A stretcher-bearer's job was to get the wounded to safety. Spicer did his job, but he did more than that. He was "the last man to seek shelter . . . while he shielded a Marine with his own body."

Do men really do this? Do they put their own lives at risk to save their comrades, even falling on grenades to do so? James Anderson Jr., a 20-year-old Marine under fire in Cam Lộ in February 1967, reached out to grasp a live grenade, and in the language of his posthumous Medal of Honor citation, "pulled it to his chest and curled around it as it went off." He was the first African American Marine to be awarded the Medal of Honor. There is a navy ship (MV *PFC James Anderson Jr.*), a park, and a street in California named for him. Larry G. Dahl served on a gun truck team operating from Quy Nhơn. In February 1971, at the top of the An Khê Pass, and after engaging the enemy, Dahl threw himself on an enemy grenade, saving the lives of his three crew members. The army awarded him the Medal of Honor posthumously. There is a navy cargo ship named for him.[22]

There is a belief that such radical self-sacrificing acts are more common in "cohesive" military units. The historian of the army's Transportation Corps wrote that gun crews "had a bond that made losing a crew member like losing a brother." In interviewing gun crew members in the wake of Dahl's death, he noted that many believed "that any crew member would have made the same sacrifice" as Dahl. No doubt that's what many believe, or better, would like to believe. But is it really plausible? Wouldn't the vast majority of us, even serving in "cohesive" military units, shrink from such self-sacrifice?[23]

Émile Durkheim's classic study of suicide offers a context for understanding self-sacrifice in the military. He argued that such acts of "altruistic suicide" were inherent in military service because a soldier was "trained to set little value upon himself since he must be prepared to sacrifice himself upon being ordered to do so." Thus he argued that noncommissioned officers—sergeants—were more likely to put themselves at risk than mere privates or officers, the latter having "a more developed individuality . . . a keener feeling of the value of his life."

Noncommissioned officers both displayed a stronger "military spirit" and were wedded by their jobs to a "habit of passive submission." Durkheim's theory of altruistic suicide in the military was a product of its time and country, a time of rigid class distinctions and a country where military discipline was enforced by firing squads. It can't explain radical self-sacrifice in the Vietnam War.[24]

Durkheim briefly alluded to a form of conscious military self-sacrifice, "what might be called heroic suicide," but he never enlarged upon it. Two American social scientists would attempt to do so by seeking to apply Durkheim's unexamined theory of "heroic suicide" to cases of soldiers falling on grenades to save their comrades. Their efforts cannot explain such singular acts, only the circumstances which make such acts more likely. But the great virtue of the articles are the empirical findings. Jeffrey W. Reimer documented 125 cases of "heroic suicide" among men awarded the Medal of Honor since its inception in the Civil War. The language of the citation makes it clear. The recipient must put his own life at risk "above and beyond the call of duty"—a supererogatory act in the language of theology. There were 260 Medals of Honor awarded in Vietnam, sixty-four (one-quarter) of them for men falling on grenades—this in a war where the vast majority of men did not train together and did not go to war together, where men grew warier of risk as they came closer to the end of their year-long tours, and where no one wanted to be the last man to die in Vietnam after President Richard Nixon made clear that we were pulling out. How can we explain this?[25]

Ray Stubbe offered an answer to a different but related question asked by Jurate Kazickas. Struggling to make sense of "war's loathsome reality," Kazickas asked Stubbe if those who died in Vietnam had died in vain. Stubbe's answer would echo down the years: "I don't think Vietnam was worth fighting for, but I cannot bring myself to say their deaths were meaningless.... These men did not die for Vietnam or Washington. They died for their friends—trying to save each other or giving of themselves to prevent others from dying. These deaths were not meaningless because they died for each other."[26]

Stubbe, a good and thoughtful pastor, trying to answer an impossible question, gave voice to a trope that would find its most persuasive expression in movies and shows such as *Band of Brothers*. "They died for each other" is at best an explanation that refuses the simplistic closures—they died for their country, for democracy, for Mom and apple pie. It's an explanation that makes some of us feel good. Those who have never been to war would like to believe that those who do become a band of brothers, maybe because there is so little brotherhood in the civilian world. There are war veterans who have retrospectively affirmed such brotherhood and may well have experienced it. Stubbe certainly did. Count me a skeptic. That wasn't my war. The army I knew in Vietnam was marked by sharp unbrotherly divisions, by rank and by race. There were "juicers" and "heads," true believers in the war and skeptical opponents, barely competent junior officers, and

CHAPTER 5

always—always, the bumbling fools who couldn't properly clear their weapons, who fell out of guard towers asleep, or who never answered a radio check and put everyone at risk. But that wasn't the whole story.

I served with one man who risked his life, not for fellow Americans but for ARVN (Army of the Republic of Vietnam) Rangers in Operation Lam Son 719 in the spring of 1971. This was Dennis M. Fujii, a helicopter crew chief in the 237th Medical Detachment, who remained for five days on an ARVN landing zone, treating the wounded, despite his own wounds, while calling in air and artillery strikes, after two attempts to rescue him failed. After the first attempt failed, he radioed his command that the landing zone was too hot for further attempts. For those five days he was the only American among ARVN rangers. At one point, he had to take up a rifle to defend the perimeter against an assault by a reinforced regiment of NVA soldiers. "There were several times I felt that I wasn't going to make it out alive." Eventually rescued, his wounds treated in Phu Bai, flown back to his home in Hawaii on compassionate leave, Fujii was awarded the army's Distinguished Service Cross, its poorly named second highest award for valor. (On 5 July 2022, in a ceremony at the White House, Dennis Fujii was awarded the Medal of Honor.)[27]

We were both members of a larger command, the 61st Medical Battalion (dustoff). The 61st had a motto that can still bring tears to my eyes: Inest Clementia Forti (Mercy is Inherent in the Brave), so different from the quotidian or sanguinary mottos of other army units. It is, of course, untrue. All armies have a full complement of brave and merciless men. Yet in its souring aspiration, Inest Clementia Forti is a motto that continues to touch my heart. Dennis Fujii fully lived up to it on those spring days in 1971.

Fujii's story and Spicer's were fully reported at the time. Numerous local papers extolled Fujii's heroism and Spicer's selfless death. But such stories were largely forgotten, as critics lavished praise on writers such as Michael Herr who told us in *Dispatches* that the war was meaningless and absurd, and Tim O'Brien who, in *The Things They Carried*, would offer his own cynical take on stories of soldiers falling on grenades to save their buddies. Do soldiers do that, O'Brien asked? "You'd feel cheated if it never happened. Without the grounding reality, it's just a trite bit of puffery, pure

Hollywood, untrue in the same way all such stories are untrue. Yet even if it did happen—and maybe it did, anything's possible—even then you know it can't be true, because a true war story does not depend on that kind of truth. Absolute occurrence is irrelevant. A thing may happen and be a total lie; another thing may not happen and be truer than the truth."[28]

O'Brien did more than any other Vietnam War writer to blur the distinction between truth and fiction. In his words directly following the passage above, he offered a fanciful story of a soldier fecklessly falling on a grenade powerful enough to kill everyone. "Before they die, though, one of the dead guys says, 'The fuck you do that for? And the jumper says, 'Story of my life, man,' and the other guy starts to smile but he's dead." O'Brien concludes: "That's a true story that never happened"—"truer than the truth." It appears that O'Brien never doubted that men risked their lives for others, but for him it was all fecklessness, lacking meaning: "Story of my life, man."[29]

O'Brien also writes: "A true war story is never moral, it does not instruct, nor encourage virtue." "You can tell a true war story by its absolute and uncompromising allegiance to obscenity and evil." It's a stance that traces back to the World War I poets Siegfried Sassoon and especially Wilfred Owen through to Ernest Hemingway—"I had seen nothing sacred, and the things that were glorious had no glory"—and would find its most powerful contemporary expression in the last works of the late scholar/veteran Paul Fussell. Writing against the "sanitized and romanticized" posturing widespread since the successful Allied conclusion of the Second World War, Fussell fixed his eye on all that was "indescribably cruel and insane," a war that could not be understood without some theory of "mass insanity and inbuilt, inherited corruption."[30]

Fussell was a contrarian ironist with a deep moral sense. However vile the war, there were acts that rose above it that were "not at all vile." O'Brien is a surrealist writing in a register that had great appeal to well-educated Americans in the aftermath of a bad war when few wanted to hear stories of courage and self-sacrifice. Fussell valued war memoir that avoided "allusion and suggestion and ironic learned comment" in preference to "an uncomplicated delivery of the facts." O'Brien once wrote such a memoir,

If I Die in a Combat Zone, but then decided to do something more "writerly," in *The Things They Carried*, more postmodern and cynical, a work that made his reputation and would have no place for the selfless actions of Jonathan Spicer.[31]

So how do we explain Spicer's act that March morning? We'll never know for sure, but we ought to recognize the context. His father said he read the Bible daily. Stubbe recalled Spicer's words: "He didn't care what happened to him; he just didn't want to hurt anyone else." Dan Sullivan recalled a longer conversation: "I'm not afraid to die, Dan. But I cannot kill anyone for any reason. It goes against all my beliefs in God and the way my family brought me up. 'Do no harm to another human being.' Killing is wrong. I honestly believe that." George Anderson told us, "He held on to that big old Bible and kept saying that no matter what we did to him he still loved us." He told his father that his fellow Marines "treated me with disdain and contempt." "Love your neighbor and pray for those who persecute you" (Matthew 5:44, New Revised Standard Version). His first sergeant told Stubbe that Spicer "won't take up his rifle and clean it and the guys are beating him up." "If anyone strikes you on the right cheek, turn the other also" (Matthew 5:39, NRSV). Spicer was, according to Ed Feldman, a Charlie Med doctor, "thoroughly unselfish and wouldn't hesitate to put himself in danger." His father offered a final word: "He had a lot of faith and lived honorably and died honorably." "No one has greater love than this, to lay down one's life for one's friends" (John 15:13, NRSV). Jonathan Spicer put his life at risk for wounded men he did not know. We need no deeper understanding, no further context to grasp the meaning of his radical self-sacrificing act on that March morning in Khe Sanh.[32]

CHAPTER 6

Three Memoirs

Ron Donahey, Cliff Roberson, and C. Michael Dingman served as CO medics in Vietnam. All would write memoirs of their time in the war, memoirs infused by an intense religious faith. Roberson and Dingman wrote in part for their families, and for posterity, though Dingman also believed that his writing had a therapeutic value; sharing what he had been through, he realized, "was my way of dealing with it, of getting it out rather than keeping it in." Donahey and Roberson were Seventh-day Adventists, though oddly Roberson never explicitly claimed membership. Dingman, whose family was not religious, came to believe in Jesus in a small evangelical Bible church while in high school. All three were from the West: Donahey from Washington, Roberson from California, Dingman from Oregon. All were high school graduates. Dingman spent a year in a Bible college; Roberson took some art classes at Mt. San Antonio College in Walnut, California.[1]

They came from modest backgrounds. Donahey was born in 1945, "not poor and not middle class."[2] From the age of ten he lived on the campus of Auburn Academy, an Adventist school where his mother was on the staff. Roberson's father worked as a printer in Northern California. Dingman's father was a baker in Gresham, Oregon. His parents were not religious. They divorced when he was a freshman in high school. His older brother was drafted into the Marines, his sister left home to marry, and his younger brother went to live with his father. He stayed with his mother, later joined by a stepdad and a younger stepsister. She would lead him to a small house church that helped to change his life.

CHAPTER 6

They came to their decisions to serve differently. Donahey was clear-eyed in 1965: "I wanted to go," he told an interviewer, that is he wanted to serve as a uniformed conscientious objector, though he preferred the term "noncombatant" over that of "objector." He knew of the heroic service of his fellow Adventist, Desmond Doss, in World War II and was inspired by it. This was what his church taught and for which Auburn Academy had prepared him. In his senior year, he took a required Medical Cadet Corps class, where he drew uniforms, learned to march, and to offer first aid.[3]

Roberson seemed to back into the draft in 1965. His course load was not sufficient for a deferment. "It was great to be alive," he wrote, "to be a 19-year-old guy who doesn't have to go to school if he doesn't want to." Then his draft notice. When he registered in San Gabriel, he told his local draft board that he would not kill or carry a gun. He offered his readers no basis for his beliefs. His draft board accommodated him. He would be classified 1-A-0 and trained as a medic.

Dingman did not belong to a pacifist church, nor did he believe that it was wrong to kill in war. But he felt Jesus was calling him to a different path. His draft board in 1968 agreed. He would serve as a noncombatant. "I had no idea what that meant," he wrote. "Little did I know that my decision would in no way keep me out of combat," he continued. "It would have quite the opposite effect, almost guaranteeing I would go to Vietnam and be assigned to an infantry unit" facing the same risks as any combat soldier.[4]

They may have differed in their degree of intention and foreknowledge in deciding to serve as noncombatants, but each made a decision rooted in a personal or religious moral code. None of them reflected on the causes, the meaning, the justice or injustice of the American war. None appeared to know at the time of the growing controversy over the war or of the passions that the war was just then beginning to arouse. In fairness, Donahey and Roberson faced their decisions early in 1965.[5]

Donahey had positive memories of basic training; the food was good, the training cadre respectful: "It was the exception . . . to hear rough or abusive language from them." (This was my experience as well. The mess hall had received several awards, and I recall one junior cook complaining that the head cook acted as if he were overseeing a restaurant.) It should not be surprising that training cadre were measured in how they treated men who had made strong moral and religious decisions, some of whom could be quite prickly in their defense.[6]

Dingman recalled basic training as his first experience with African Americans: "Here I was living, eating, and training with people of all races," a common experience of military training since the world wars. What was uncommon to military training and was distinctive to CO basic is that he was among people of faith, and "our faith provided a basis for friendship."[7]

Yet the specter of orders to Vietnam weighed on him, as it did so many others. Dingman and I were in basic training at the same time, the summer of 1969. I wrote about how the specter of orders to Vietnam weighed on me in "*War Stories.*" Rumors were rife. He heard that they were only sending volunteers. He had hopes, which he confided to his parents, that he would be assigned to Germany or to a stateside unit. It was not to be. It nearly broke his faith: "Lord, why should I even be a Christian if this is the way You are going to treat me?" He tells us he quickly recovered. His faith in Jesus "gave purpose and meaning" to his life. He could not give Jesus up.[8]

The likelihood of Vietnam service weighed even more heavily on Roberson. His writing about this time is an odd mixture of adolescent humor, denial, and dread. Dread predominates. His deepest fear is becoming a prisoner tortured by the Viet Cong. While playing cards, he remarks that the ace of spades, with its association with death, is an "appropriate symbol right now with Vietnam hanging over my head." A class on field dressing has an "ominous ring." A trip to the Alamo, given its history of being overrun, "is not too good for morale." He signs up for the Whitecoat program (open only to Adventists and thus the evidence that he is an Adventist). "I realize this is a desperate thing to do," he writes, "to sign up to be a guinea pig and let the Army experiment on me . . . but I am desperate." He wasn't selected. His grand hope is that he will serve in England or Germany. It wasn't to be.[9]

He had his orders for Vietnam. His mother feels that her "world has been torn apart." Vietnam "hangs over his head like a black cloud." *"What is going to happen to me,"* he wrote. *"How did I get into this mess"* (italics in original). His father and brother drove him to the Oakland Army Terminal

CHAPTER 6

on 2 January 1967: "When we got to the terminal, we said our last good byes. I tried to be brave, but I felt like crying."[10]

Ron Donahey made lasting friendships in basic training among his fellow Adventists. Most of his basic class also went through medical training together. He had orders, along with ten of his friends, to the 2nd Battalion, 8th Infantry of the 4th Infantry Division, then in training for Vietnam, at Fort Lewis, Washington, and just thirty-five miles from his home. His home became a Sabbath retreat for his Adventist friends, "our own serviceman's center in her home," according to his friend Ruben D. Martinez. Dorothy Donahey embraced cooking for as many as twenty of these young Adventist medics, and she would maintain a shared correspondence with fifteen, offering Christian council and hope, all of whom would serve in Vietnam. There is a picture of eight men in summer tans, perhaps taken at Donahey's house. Ron, wearing glasses and appearing taller than his friends, has been singled out. Another soldier, perhaps Martinez, has made sure that the single chevron, then denoting promotion to Private First Class (PFC), was visible on Donahey's right arm. Though Donahey chose not to mention it, his promotion was evidence of his having graduated near the top of his basic training class. He was the only PFC in the group.[11]

In the early years of the war, it was not uncommon for whole units that had trained together to be deployed together. This was the case for the first Marine units that arrived in Đà Nẵng in 1965 as evidenced in Philip Caputo's *A Rumor of War*, and for elements of the First Cavalry Division who would fight the first major battle of the war in the Ia Drang Valley in the same year, a battle searingly evoked in Harold G. Moore's and Joseph L. Galloway's *We Were Soldiers Once . . . and Young*. In these early years, before the futility of the war bred anger and disillusion, men went to war with a certain élan. For Caputo, this was our "splendid little war." Perhaps he really believed it, but it was a trope that would of course give way to its opposite—war as the purest form of irony. Donahey would sail to Vietnam with the first elements of the Fourth Infantry Division arriving in Quy Nhơn, and later in Pleiku in the Central Highlands (II Corps) in the summer of 1966.[12]

Roberson arrived in Vietnam in January 1967 and learned that he was assigned to the 1st Battalion of the 2nd Infantry, First Infantry Division in

Phước Vĩnh in III Corps. Dingman came to Vietnam in December 1969 and was assigned to the 3rd Battalion, 506th Infantry, 101st Airborne Division in Phu Bai, I Corps in the north of the country. All three, like so many young soldiers and Marines, were struck by the strangeness of the country and its people.

"Walking off the plane was like walking into another world," Dingman wrote. "I was immediately taken aback by the poverty of the Vietnamese people," he went on. Except for a mission trip to Mexico, he had never been to a third-world country. His comments were echoed by Roberson and Donahey. "I saw people in . . . dirty clothes. They had dirty houses and dirty yards," the latter wrote. He told his parents: "This sure is a dumpy place." Donahey found himself among people whose poverty he had never encountered and whose habits shocked him, Vietnamese women and children "fishing around in the slop," the food waste Americans were throwing out, a woman urinating beside the road, another next to him in a Pleiku outhouse, his thought: "I wondered what my mom would think." In encountering such difference, Donahey gave voice to a crude but all too typical American judgment. That woman urinating by the side of the road looked up with her "toothless beetle [betel] nut grin." The "air" of Pleiku "was filled with the stench of unwashed bodies and stagnant water." The primitive highland tribesmen, called Montagnards by the French (shortened to "Yards" by Americans) with their loincloths were a people out of the "stone age." His only reference point for understanding was "the pictures missionaries would show in church."[13]

Yet in fairness to Donahey, he also proved capable of kindness and compassion: buying a new shirt for a Vietnamese boy who had cleaned his boots, treating a tribesman who had malaria and who had been so moved that he took a bracelet off his wrist and gave it to Donahey as an emblem of lasting friendship. The gesture moved Donahey to tears, though he was glad that it was too dark for his new friend to see them.

Every CO medic, once arriving in Vietnam, would face the same question—would they take a weapon? All three decided that they would not, at least initially. Only Dingman wrote about it. He recalled being pressured by his company commander to do so. He chose not to and found himself on

CHAPTER 6

fatigue duty while the rest of his training class was at the firing range. I faced no such pressure and accompanied my fellow soldiers to the firing range where I paid close attention to the loading, aiming, and firing of M16s, a skill I was thankful I never had to practice.

Donahey went even further in his efforts to uphold Adventist theology and practice. The Adventist Sabbath is Saturday, and SDA leadership worked closely with the army to ensure that their soldiers could observe the day. At Fort Lewis, Donahey and others objected to a Saturday order to begin processing for Vietnam. A phone call to a senior SDA elder led to further calls down the chain of command. The young soldiers prevailed. Once in Vietnam, however, a similar refusal to fill sandbags on the Sabbath provoked the ire of senior officers. He and his fellow Adventists had no objection to performing medical duty on the Sabbath—Jesus healed on the Sabbath after all—but not routine fatigue duty. Donahey, fearing prolonged KP and guard duty, requested a transfer from the relative safety of the Headquarters Company to a line company. He joined Alpha Company where he became the medic to the weapons platoon.

Once assigned to an infantry platoon as unarmed medics, neither Donahey nor Dingman reported any hostility or lack of acceptance. CO medics were not numerous, but they were not uncommon. They were not assigned directly to infantry companies. They reported instead to the battalion surgeon whose staff would detail them to companies in need of medics and who would likely make clear to company commanders that some of their medics did not carry weapons. It should have been no surprise then when CO medics reported. Roberson's experience was different, however. He reported that his platoon leader called him names and mocked him in front of his men. But he didn't know why, though he speculated that, likely correctly, it was because he carried a Bible rather than an M16 or a .45.

The three brought a deep religious sensibility to their service. Donahey believed in signs and portents and in an active, protective God. Prior to his embarkation, he bought a .22 to protect himself from snakes. When it blew up in his hand in target practice, he decided that God had told him he didn't need it: "I was at peace about my safety." Later, in an operation near the Cambodian border, he witnessed the crash of an American helicopter.

He moved to assist the crew, dazed but alive. Upon returning he saw a part of the helicopter's tail rotor embedded near where he had been sitting: "Again, I realized the protection I had just received and its Source." Why him, and why not others? If he ever thought deeply about it, he chose not to write about it.[14]

Roberson, while on patrol, silently sang a hymn: "Anywhere with Jesus I can safely go. Anywhere He leads me in this world below." When he learned that a nearby unit had suffered seventeen killed, he asked the difficult question that Donahey hadn't: "If Almighty God watches over me, does He have to ignore others to do it?" Dingman's letters home reassured his family that God was watching over him. "God has been and is with me," he wrote in one letter. "He had to be to allow me to still be here." Every chapter in his book contains a Biblical verse as epigraph. "I have often told people if it were not my faith in God," he wrote, "I don't think I could have made it through my year in Vietnam."[15]

All three men would soon face combat, but Donahey, Roberson, and Dingman would quickly come to learn that their lives were at risk not just from the enemy but from the carelessness of fellow soldiers. Roberson, who would write *"I'm not ready to be a medic"* (italics in the original), treated sprained ankles and self-inflicted injuries. The worst was a soldier who died from his own grenade. The soldier had straightened the cotter pin that holds the handle in place, the pin normally bent for safety reasons, in order to arm it more quickly. Donahey experienced similar deaths—two drunken NCOs arguing over how to use a Claymore mine. Then the accidents, a soldier wounding himself with a grenade launcher, another walking into the rotating propellor of a C-130, and another killed when the muzzle of an artillery piece burst. The worst, a point man killing a fellow soldier he failed to recognize. Some years later, as I was queuing for my orders to the 4th Infantry, a kindly and elderly sergeant, likely all of 35, said to me: "Watch out, son, they're shooting themselves up there." Dingman recalled that the failure to retrieve and disarm a Claymore mine cost his point man, Mike Kosky, his leg.[16]

CHAPTER 6

In October 1966, Donahey saw his first sustained combat. Ordered with his platoon to assist an embattled Bravo Company, he arrived in the afternoon. Settling in to a foxhole, he began to smell the nauseating odor of the decaying bodies of NVA troops, "an odor I had never smelled before." Under attack at night, he heard the cry for a medic. He moved forward, refusing the offer of a .45 from his lieutenant. The wounded soldier was a machine gunner and he warned Donahey that his assailant was still close by. Donahey patched a hip wound and gave the soldier a shot of morphine but needed help in dragging him back to safety. Returning to his lines, he found a volunteer and they brought the wounded soldier back. His lieutenant, he tells us, put him in for the Bronze Star. In the book's conclusion, Donahey recounts his successful effort to find and reconnect with the soldier, Preston Leaderbrand, who assisted him. They never identified the wounded machine gunner.[17]

Donahey now realized that he was in a "real war." The next morning, walking among the NVA dead, he looked at a face and "saw the horror of violence, not the peace he should have had." Going through his belongings, and recognizing the humanity of one of his enemies, he saw the photograph of a mother and child, a half-written letter, a shaving kit, his "last earthly possessions," "his family would never know what happened to him . . . only that he never returned from the war."[18]

Donahey's war would grind on through Tet, 1967. Called to assist a platoon of Charlie Company, he arrived to learn that most had died, more than twenty: "Death! You get immune to seeing it, you learn to control your emotions, but it never quite goes away. You see the broken bodies and you smell the odor of death. It no longer causes physical sickness, but it is always there to remind you of what war is about." Two R&R leaves and occasional duty in the rear would prove respites. Through it all, he sought to remain in contact with the fellow Adventists he had trained with and whom his mother fed on Sabbath Saturdays.[19]

Donahey had gone to war with men he knew and with whom he trained. Most had been wounded. One had died. This was William Allen Gilmore from Oklahoma City, who died in Kon Tum Province 21 February 1967. Donahey's book is dedicated to him. His picture next to the copyright page contains the verse from John 15:13, "Greater love has no one than this, than to lay down one's life for his friends." Ruben Martinez, a friend and fellow Adventist, invoking those Sabbath dinners, would post on Gilmore's Wall of Faces site, "Hi Allen, it's us. your Mrs. Donahey Family."[20]

Donahey retained his commitment to core Adventist principles as best he could, and with a certain good humor. Trading ham and lima beans C-rations for "something a little more vegetarian," trading a can of beer for two of pop. He surprised his fellow soldiers with his facility with weapons. When volatile aviation fuel rolled off a truck and had to be destroyed, Donahey picked up a grenade launcher and did the job. But a tree partially deflected the grenade and a small piece of shrapnel hit the truck driver—so he became, in his words, "the Conscientious Objector who wouldn't kill the enemy but had no objection to wounding his own buddies."[21]

More seriously, he found himself on two occasions with weapons in his hand on patrol. Half of his fellow Adventists had taken up weapons. "I did not want to be put in a situation to have to kill anyone," he wrote, but "If it came down to kill or be killed, I would kill." That thought led to Donahey's taking up the offer of his battalion surgeon to serve out his time in the battalion aid station. There is a picture of him at the aid station, looking thoughtful, his hair close-cropped, his thinness noticeable. He's wearing stateside fatigues, not the jungle fatigues that would later become standard. He's been promoted to Specialist Fourth Class, the rank visible on his left arm.[22]

A month into his tour, Roberson faced his first call for a medic. His squad leader, Sgt. Willie Tyler, had been shot. "I took off crawling as near to the ground as I could get," but he lost his aid bag on the way and had to go back for it. Tyler was then shot a second time, this time in the chest—a sucking chest wound. Roberson tried to seal the entry wound as he had been trained to do, but he failed to see the larger exit would. He was distraught: "*Did I do all I could? Did I do everything right?*"(italics in original). He blames his training: "Why didn't they teach me more about sucking chest wounds? Why didn't they stress more about battle wounds?" Willie Tyler from Leland, Mississippi, the prior recipient of a Silver Star and a Bronze Star for Valor, died that day, the first of March 1967.[23]

CHAPTER 6

Roberson remained in the field for another six months uneventfully but for a bizarre lightning strike. In the midst of a monsoon rain, he was struck by lightning. The lightning hit a tree with attached commo wire linked to a radio in the bunker he was in. He had no idea what was happening. He later learned that a sergeant found him face down in water and not breathing. The sergeant performed CPR and Roberson rallied and, except for a bout of vomiting, there were no lingering aftereffects. "Sparks" was his new nickname. He would later regale his daughters about the night that he died in Vietnam.[24]

On July 4, he learned that he would be assigned to the battalion aid station in Phước Vĩnh. "Things look very good for me," he wrote. "I spent six months out in the field—six months of patrol, digging bunkers, and radio watch—six months of almost constant stress... never knowing when I might hear that dreaded cry, 'Medic!' Now it's over." He was now safer, but the trauma of war continued. Fourteen days later, he learned that the medic who replaced him, Tony Ribera, had died in an attack that killed six others, including the platoon leader who had mocked him. Ribera, from Raton, New Mexico, was a thirty-year-old PFC who, it was rumored, had a doctorate in psychology and who could have been an officer but chose to be a medic. Ribera was awarded the Silver Star posthumously. Roberson didn't mention the award and may not have known about it. But he was wrenched by Ribera's death:

> I lived
> Tony died
> Why[25]

Working in a battalion aid station was no guarantee against death. In October, a VC ambush required the battalion surgeon, Cpt. Howard Gerstal, and a medic, Don Schrenk, to leave the aid station to offer assistance to the growing number of wounded. Both were killed. Gerstal was Roberson's boss in the aid station; Schrenk, a fellow Adventist, was Roberson's friend. Both were married and had children, children "that will never know their fathers."[26]

Roberson's war was soon to be over. He had experienced combat and the death of men he knew. He remained loyal to his conscience but recognized that he would have used a weapon to protect his fellow soldiers, though he didn't "want to think about things like that." He would return from the war with a Bronze Star for Valor (for his efforts to save Sgt. Willie Tyler), stories of racial tension, fragging incidents, as well as the apocryphal stories that circulated among credulous young soldiers, prisoners thrown from helicopters, the bamboo viper that would kill you in seconds, the hideous torture that the VC visited upon American prisoners, even prisoners that somehow survived to die in the arms of Americans. He also came back with ringworm on his right ankle, exacerbated by a leech bite, that he could never get rid of: "It haunts me to this day, just like my memories of the Vietnam War."[27]

Mike Dingman would face combat within a week of his joining Delta Company. At the base of Hill 474 in southern Bình Điền Province, his platoon was ambushed by NVA who held higher ground. Victor San Nicholas, nicknamed Guam because that was where he was from, was the first hit: gut shot with a small exit wound. Dingman applied compresses over both wounds and made clear to the platoon leader that they would need a medevac. A squad was sent to secure a landing zone (LZ) in a meadow below them. Dingman, Benjamin Garcia, and two others began to carry Guam to the LZ when Garcia was hit, his body tumbling down the trail. Then the cry "Medic" from the meadow. Jeff Miller was shot in the head; another soldier, Smitty, in the thigh. He would make it, but Miller would not. Nor would Garcia, who was hit on the right side of his chest. Dingman later came to think, based on the bullet's trajectory and his position opposite Garcia's, that the round had been meant for him. His overall narrative is replete with his belief that God was watching over him. But he had the grace to leave that belief unmentioned in his account of the death of Benjamin Garcia.[28]

The platoon's travail was only beginning. Three medevac missions encountering heavy enemy fire all aborted. A pilot and a crew chief were hit. One helicopter was declared a total loss. As the platoon tried to find better fighting positions, Sgt. George Spillers took a bullet in his forehead, dying immediately. The platoon leader, along with Sgt. Rudy Boykins, a Black squad leader, tried to carry Guam once again to safety. NVA fire wounded

CHAPTER 6

Boykins in the right elbow and hit Guam again, this time in the face and head. He would not survive. Boykins's wound bled profusely and Dingman applied a tourniquet. As night approached, the remaining platoon members formed a defensive perimeter in the meadow.[29]

The morning found them short of water and other supplies. Under fire and maneuvering for safety the day before, men had left their rucksacks behind. Dingman woke up that morning to find his hands coated in the dried blood of the dead and wounded. The platoon needed to get off the meadow and find an escape route down the mountain. Sergeant Schrang found a small stream about fifty meters away. The stream would replenish their water and covered by brush offer an escape route. But they would have to crawl to it. But Rudy Boykins, with a damaged arm bloated by the tourniquet, could not crawl.

Dingman placed Boykins on his back secured by a utility belt that encircled them both. But the tightness of the belt prevented a weakened Boykins from breathing. There were no good options. They called for a fourth medevac mission. One of the pilots from the day before (CWO Michael Haeusserman), unable to sleep knowing that he had not been able to retrieve the wounded, volunteered to form a crew. Dingman rigged a stretcher using a shirt and two M16s and with three others successfully carried Boykins to the evacuation point. The medevac, flying low to avoid detection, completed the mission, though not without substantial damage, rendering it unflyable.

The platoon was now able to follow the original plan. It would take them two days, assisted by a helicopter resupply, to finally find safety. "We had been beaten badly," Dingman wrote, "and suffered terrible loss." Dingman had come to understand war viscerally: "I had seen, heard, and tasted it. . . . I had the blood of the wounded and the dead on my hands. I was no longer the new guy. . . . I was a grunt, a soldier." He had chosen to carry an extra M16 on the platoon's retreat. Did he want to turn it in, his platoon leader asked? He chose to keep it. Recommended for the award of the Silver Star, higher authority downgraded it to the Bronze Star for Valor. There was no award ceremony. He received the medal as he was processing out of the army. A clerk "pulled the medal from a glass cabinet like you would candy in a theater."[30]

Dingman remained in the field for eight months, the extra two months because of a shortage of medics. In the spring of 1970, his unit proved to be a lead element of the invasion of Cambodia. He patrolled both Tiger Mountain and the Crow's Foot area, among other places, facing fear, anxiety, fatigue, but he never experienced the sustained combat of his first weeks in Vietnam. He went out of his way to stay in touch with men who had been wounded, especially Rudy Boykins, who lost his arm because of the tourniquet and the delay in evacuating him. Rudy wrote back wanting to thank Dingman "for doing everything you did while I was wounded . . . without your help and God's I probably wouldn't be here, especially keeping me awake all night." The tourniquet kept him from bleeding out and likely saved his life.[31]

Ron Donahey returned to Washington state to work in sales, married, and had two daughters. At the age of forty-three he decided to attend college. That led to a Master of Social Work degree, and a job with the Veterans Administration where he treated fellow Vietnam veterans, diagnosed with PTSD. He retired in 2004, when "my own PTSD hit me." He never elaborated further in print.[32]

He would tell more in a recent interview. He returned home. His nightmares receded, but he couldn't sleep. He didn't know what was wrong. There was then no notion of something called PTSD. When he began counseling Vietnam veterans with PTSD, he insisted he did not suffer from it, but he began to recognize the signs, immersed as he was in counseling. He came to know that he had it, and then a second blow. At fifty, he learned that he had type 2 diabetes linked to exposure to Agent Orange. The VA granted him a 100 percent disability. All of his fellow SDA medics had either PTSD or diabetes.[33]

Ron Donahey, as a recent YouTube interview attests, remains a handsome, friendly, open man, with a full head of hair neatly combed. His religious beliefs shine through. He remains a committed Adventist hoping to meet God in heaven. His refusal to kill in war was religious and not at all political. He came to know the depth of opposition to the Vietnam War only after he came home. His only protest was purely and oddly personal.

CHAPTER 6

One day he took his uniform out of the closet, cut it into small pieces, and burned it, saving only his Combat Medic Badge, an image of which graces the cover of his book.[34]

Cliff Roberson came home to Jenny, a college classmate of his sister who had encouraged her to write to her brother. They were married in January 1969. Jenny trained as a nurse and gave birth to two daughters. Cliff, by his own account, struggled through "dead end jobs," returned to the printing business and worked for his father for a time, and later sold hanging planter pots. None of this was remunerative and he more than once found himself in conflict with his bosses. In 1977, they moved to Northern Idaho and built a log cabin during the "Big Back to Nature–Live Off the Land–Eat Pine Cones craze," as he put it. Two years later, convinced that after his army experience he did not trust anyone in authority and thus could not work for others, he opened his own print shop.[35]

Then one morning, "I beat my oldest daughter and smashed the TV" because she had refused to eat the breakfast his wife had prepared. "All the rage inside me," he wrote, "broke loose." It was not the first time he had had "irrational explosions of anger." He never tells his readers exactly why. Most of his writing in these pages records his frustrations and humiliations in forging a civilian career. A careful reader might conclude those trials were sufficient cause for his anger. Yet that's not what he wanted to believe. In the lead-up to his story of rage he makes clear that he felt disrespected for his service, a common feeling for many veterans, that his service made him different (reinforced by the movies "portraying Vietnam vets as crazy psychos"), and then sweepingly: "How could I have known how Vietnam would color and shape the rest of my life—that the boy who went to Vietnam would never come home."[36]

He reconciled with his wife and daughter, moved back to California in 1986, and established a new printing business. At church, he met two fellow veterans, and a visit in 1988 to the California Vietnam Veterans Memorial in Sacramento, and two years later to the Wall in Washington, DC, brought healing and pride. Then a visit to the National Archives to examine the records of his unit (some of which are included in his book) "brought to the surface stuff that I had repressed from my subconscious." He tells us nothing further. The records he cites are terse, minute-by-minute duty officers' logs from brigade headquarters. His annotations highlight the days Tyler, Ribera, Gerstal, and Schrenk died.[37]

His printing business suffered, as computerized printing became increasingly common. His health deteriorated. He suffered panic attacks and nightmares linked to the war. Visits to the VA resulted in a 30 percent disability in 1999. A friend from church offered a lifeline, a job as a shop teacher for mentally challenged kids. The job paid him more per hour than he had ever made. A bad back forced his resignation. Then another round with the VA. With his wife's help ("She told the VA everything I had denied to myself.... She laid my whole miserable life out on the table") he was granted full disability in 2005.[38]

Mike Dingman returned home in the fall of 1970 and served out his two-year commitment at Fort Lewis, Washington, mustering out on 28 May 1971. Once again, we overlapped. I left the army from Fort Lewis on May Day, 1971. He returned to work at a children's home in Hollywood, California, where he had worked prior to being drafted, while reconnecting with Barbara, a woman he had known and with whom he corresponded during the war. They were married in June 1972. He entered full-time ministry in 1978 in the Pacific Northwest, much later traveling east for a degree at Lancaster Bible College in Pennsylvania. Since 2007, he has been Associate Pastor at the Great Bridge Evangelical Free Church in Virginia Beach, Virginia, with a special mission to the area's veterans.[39]

When Dingman first came home he had frequent nightmares and became agitated when helicopters flew over. He made models of helicopters as therapy. "Over time all of these symptoms dissipated," he wrote, "in part, I am convinced, because I have been able to talk about my experiences in the context of ministry, sharing the lessons God taught me on the battlefield." In a later email, he clarified that he knew his symptoms were congruent with what only later came to be recognized as PTSD, but he wrote, "I never really thought it as something that should debilitate me or keep me from functioning fully in personal life or professionally. Nor did I think of it as something that the government owed me for. I simply saw the effects of the war as a cost of my service."[40]

Sometime later, after suffering from tinnitus and hearing loss, he went to a VA hospital hoping only for hearing aids. He also agreed to be evaluated for PTSD. A counselor asked him the dates he had experienced intense trauma and the names of three of his fellow soldiers—easy questions. He had his book with him. He was then asked a series of other questions about nightmares, sleep patterns, his experience in large social gatherings. His answers clearly fit some of the characteristics of PTSD. A few weeks later, and to his "great surprise," he learned that the VA had granted him a 50 percent disability for PTSD. Initially denied his claim for hearing loss, he appealed, offering detailed evidence, and received an additional 10 percent.[41]

Donahey, Roberson, and Dingman had much in common. They were typical of CO medics in these years. Their dissent was religious and not at all political. They all experienced intense combat. They all came to suffer from PTSD. Donahey and Roberson acknowledged it. Dingman went deeper. He was able to talk about it in ministry, to write about it. Recall his words: "I never really thought it as something that should debilitate me or keep me from functioning fully in personal life or professionally."

His is a story of resilience, a strong and fitting coda to the tragedy of war.

CHAPTER 7

Stories of Courage and Loss

Ken Kays

Kenneth Kays arrived in Vietnam in the middle of April 1970. He was a medic and a conscientious objector, though his status as a CO had never been officially recognized by the Selective Service System or by the army. He did not carry a weapon. Assigned to the 101st Airborne Division in Thừa Thiên Province, he experienced combat on his first night in-country. "They put me in the field early," he told a reporter. "I didn't really think I was ready to take care of wounded men. But we were hit almost every night in the field, so I learned quickly."[1]

On the 5th of May, Kays, now assigned to Delta Company, 1st Battalion, 506th Infantry of the 101st Airborne Division, took part in a combat assault on an old firebase, Maureen. Kays's 2nd Platoon was in contact that day. After patrolling on the 6th, the platoon returned to Maureen to set up a night defensive position. Sappers attacked shortly before dawn on the 7th. Kays, responding to the call for a medic, moved from his foxhole to the perimeter. A satchel charge landing near him blew off the lower portion of his left leg. After applying a tourniquet, he continued to treat a wounded soldier, dragging him to a safer position. Returning to the perimeter, he treated another soldier, "using his own body as a shield," in the words of his valor citation, and moved him to safety. Finally he moved beyond the perimeter to treat another soldier in enemy territory. He later told a friend that he thought "after my leg was blown off and I could see the enemy running everywhere around us, that I was going to die. For some reason a great sense of peace came over me with this thought and I decided I would

CHAPTER 7

just go out there and help all the people I could before I died." He was not found until first light, his body protecting two wounded soldiers. Weak from loss of blood, he refused to be evacuated until those he had been treating were. For his actions that night, then Pvt. Kenneth M. Kays was awarded the Medal of Honor, in the hallowed words of the award "for conspicuous gallantry and intrepidity in action at the risk of his life above and beyond the call of duty."[2]

Ken Kays had not come easily to that moment. Born in 1949 in Mount Vernon, Illinois, and raised in nearby Fairfield, he was the only child of John and Ethel Kays, the father a World War II veteran who owned a grocery store, the mother a secretary for the local Chamber of Commerce and an insurance saleswoman. He was, according to a friend, a "high-energy person with a great sense of humor." Another friend remembered him as "a sensitive, artistic, humorous intellectual." He played chess, lifted weights, set up a darkroom for his photography, and joined the football team and the school band, two activities that rarely attracted the same person. He evidenced a rebellious streak, responding to a teacher's complaint that his hair was too long by turning up the next day with his head shaved. As the folk scene emerged nationally, he took up the guitar and began to play and sing at a local club in 1967, the year of his high school graduation. "Where Have All the Flowers Gone?" was a favorite.[3]

He enrolled at Southern Illinois University (SIU) in 1967. Just like so many other universities in those years, SIU experienced student rebellion over free speech, parietal hours, and especially the Vietnam War, rebellion severe enough to lead to the burning of Old Main in June 1969, the oldest building on the campus and home to the ROTC rifle range among other offices and classrooms. There is no evidence that Kays joined any of the radical groups on campus, Students for a Democratic Society (SDS) or the Southern Illinois Peace Committee, but by the summer of 1968, while working construction for a local farmer, Robert "Pud" Williams, he gave voice to his beliefs. Williams recalled Kays saying he "wouldn't carry a gun and didn't know whether he would accept his draft notice." He would soon face that choice, after flunking out in the spring of 1969, likely a product of his increasing drug use. A friend later put it, "We both seemed to major in the sixties, he proved the more dedicated and dropped out to devote serious attention to the connoisseurship of drugs."[4]

While waiting for his draft notice, Kays and two of his friends drove east in August to attend the music festival at Woodstock, New York. One of those friends, David Steiner, wrote a piece for the *Wayne County Press*. It was, he wrote, the "wildest week I ever experienced," noting the colorful costumes, nude swimming, the widespread use of drugs: "They were smoking marijuana and consuming acid and speed pills without reservation. Drugs were being sold as openly as hot dogs at a baseball game." Ken Kays was in his element, and his memories of Woodstock would become all he could talk about well into his army service. The community backlash, measured by letters to the editor, was severe. A second article, authored by "Fairfield Boy," likely Kays, chided the community for its hypocrisy. Bootleg liquor was just as dangerous as drugs, the article asserted. War protesters were seen as bums, but "what is so heroic about fighting for something you don't believe in? Is a person who is deferred from the draft because of medical school or teaching any better than a conscientious objector who is deferred?"[5]

His draft notice came in the middle of October. He requested conscientious objector status, 1-A-0, indicating his willingness to serve as an unarmed medic. We know nothing of his religious background or that of his parents. A copy of his application on Selective Service Form 150 apparently does not survive. There is some indication that he came to embrace Eastern religions, Hinduism and Buddhism, while at SIU. His draft board denied his request, and there is no record of its denial. We can only speculate why. If he based his application on his belief in Eastern religions, it may have been difficult for a board likely made up of conventional Baptists and Methodists to grasp his sincerity. And then there was his rebellious streak, the trip to Woodstock, the rumors of drug use likely well known in a small community of fewer than 6,000.[6]

Now faced with a hard moral decision, Kays left Illinois for Canada. He was there for less than a month. His father, using whatever local influence he had, had worked out a compromise. If Ken came home and went through basic training, the army would then train him as a medic. It would then be his choice, if assigned to Vietnam, to carry a weapon. He agreed. A friend

CHAPTER 7

speculated that Kays joined the army "because he didn't want his daddy to have to go to the coffee shop and deal with all the negative crap." Kays told the same friend, "Maybe as a medic I can help somebody."[7]

And help he did. Of the twenty-one members of 2nd Platoon more than a dozen were wounded, some of whom he helped—seven died. In addition to Kays, three men were awarded medals for valor. Kays's war on the ground was over. But the war in his head would continue. He would have been treated first at a field hospital in I Corps, eventually convalescing at Fitzsimmons General Hospital in Denver, now fitted with an artificial limb and a full array of veterans' benefits. He returned home eight months after the battle on Maureen.[8]

In January 1971, he learned that he had been awarded the Distinguished Service Cross (DSC); the poorly named medal is the army's second highest award for valor. The local paper interviewed a bearded Kays "who sat quietly in his mother's living room puffing nervously on a cigarette." He talked of what he might do next, none of which happened. He chose to go back to SIU, joined a writing class, and began to write poetry, some evidencing his drug use. The most disturbing was a reflection on that night at Maureen.

Writing to a presumed girlfriend, he wrote:

> I've seen too much and been too far
> To really love you when you're near
> For horrible visions haunt my mind
> Of bloody death and unchained fear.
> When I hold you in my arms
> I see men who've long since gone
> Guys who helped me through the night
> Blown away before the dawn.
> To men who've shared a bloody hill
> And soaked up fire and lead
> Many words acquire a new meaning
> Like love and friend and God and death
> These guys are all real as you
> And now I see that I've died too.

He would soon drop out of SIU.⁹

In October 1973, Kays learned that his award of the DSC had been upgraded to the Medal of Honor. He did not take it well. His father recalled "about the time Kenny got that medal, he stopped talking to me and his mother. He started raising hell and smoking grass." He didn't want to go to the award ceremony at the White House. "Pud" Williams convinced him to go. He refused to cut his hair or his beard, so the army refused to allow him to wear a uniform. He was the only one that day out of uniform. He was also the only one who refused to stand when President Richard Nixon entered the room. His father thought that he treated the ceremony as a "joke." Coming home, he refused the entreaties of the local press and hid for three weeks in a cabin in the woods, confiding to a friend, "I can't handle being a hero. I just don't think that I've been that brave. Besides being a Medal of Honor man doesn't make me any better than anyone else." These are not uncommon thoughts for those awarded valor medals. Often, the common refrain was that they felt they were just doing their job. Modesty in the face of a valor award is a virtue, a recognition that others, not in the same glare, were often overlooked. But Kenny Kays was taking his understandable modesty, if that was what it was, to a far darker place.¹⁰

In April 1974, police officers found marijuana growing in a small greenhouse next to John Kays's house. Ken Kays earned a fine and a year's probation. A week later, police came back and found more. Kays was defiant, telling a judge he "would keep on growing it." In June, police found more growing on a 1,000-square-foot patch of ground, owned by his father, two miles from Fairfield. The national press noticed: AP's reporter tried to explain: "At the heart of Kays's philosophy is the belief that a man must be true to himself, must do what he thinks is right. But first he must be free to find himself. . . . Marijuana is a tool in the quest. He won't participate in a system that obstructs the search." For most reporters the lazy frame of the war hero turned hippie protester, whose "long sun-tinted hair" was secured by a headband, proved irresistible. For Kays the issue was black and white: "No man has the right to dictate to another." But why did he court such intense public drama? If he just wanted to smoke grass as he had in high school and at SIU, he could have.¹¹

CHAPTER 7

On Memorial Day, 1974, he took his father's car and tore through the town shouting and honking his horn. A few days later, construction workers heard him shouting inside his trailer. His father found him screaming incoherently and agreed to commit him for medical treatment. Kays seemed to agree and committed himself in mid-June to a state mental health center in Anna, Illinois. It would be the first of five visits to that center. His mother reported that he had begun writing apologies to the dead soldiers he had tried to save "for not having reached them quickly enough." The notes were never sent. It's not clear that he even knew all their names, he had been with them so briefly. He later told a friend that "survivor's guilt is worse than any pain I felt in my leg." Survivor guilt is real and so too the guilt of medics who could not save their comrades. The best answer would have come from a thoughtful veteran, reminding Kays of how briefly he had been in-country and just how little training he had had. Whether Kays had the benefit of such advice is unknown.[12]

In the spring of 1976, a reporter from *The Daily Illini* visited the Kays and authored a devastating portrait. He met Ken's father first, a man with missing and broken teeth, tending a greenhouse, now his sole business. He had been encouraging his son to get out more, to meet with old friends. The writer learned that the son had been diagnosed, after those five visits to a mental hospital, as a "clinically depressed schizophrenic."

Ken was still in bed "sitting up in a metal cot in a darkened room.... He sits naked, rocking back and forth incessantly, his head, neck, and shoulders puffy, perhaps from the heavy dosage of Thorazine and Prolixin he's been receiving over the past few years."

The writer went on: "His hair is short now and he's balding prematurely. Thick black-framed glasses are held in place by puffy cheeks, and his eyes seem to bulge in their sockets. He doesn't look old, or young. But he certainly doesn't look twenty-six. The room is filled with books on Eastern religion and philosophy, contrasted with old issues of *Playboy*. A Whole Earth Flag hangs on the wall, his Distinguished Service Award framed nearby. His artificial leg, wrapped in dirty pants, lies on the floor." And then finally: "Ken Kays sees no future. His wrists are scarred from suicide attempts. He calls himself a Christian mystic and thinks that he is the 'third eye' (the eye of higher consciousness in Hinduism and Buddhism). When he watches television, he communicates with the people on the screen as well as others watching the program. But he doesn't watch TV anymore."[13]

This isn't just the portrait of a man who lived through a traumatic night in Vietnam, or more precisely it isn't only the result of that night that can explain what Kenny Kays had become. A few years later, Kays was found screaming at a neighbor, threw a flowerpot through the neighbor's glass door, and stole the neighbor's car. Taken into custody by force, he "allegedly tore up his mattress and set fire to it." He was declared unfit to stand trial and remanded to the Illinois Department of Mental Health, where he would stay from 1979 to 1985.[14]

His mother, suffering from a lingering illness, died in 1981, a suicide. His 74-year-old father, suffering from cancer, took Ken back home in 1985. After listening to his father's complaints about his illness, his son supposedly said: "There's a gun in the next room. If you feel that way why don't you just shoot yourself." His father did. Ken Kays lived for another six years, living alone and smoking pot daily. Over Thanksgiving weekend 1991, Kays hanged himself using a coat hanger attached to a wall-mounted bookcase. His Medal of Honor remains missing.[15]

Suicide is a great mystery. Was it that night on Maureen? Was it the Medal of Honor? "I can't handle being a hero," he said. Other men have survived battle trauma and overcome the sense of unworthiness that the highest valor medals may elicit. Was it the long years of drug taking, or even the generous disability benefits that precluded his having to work, to get on with his life? The trauma of war will always remain the easy answer. But is it enough to explain his extraordinary descent into self-destructive mental illness? Better to remember his actions that night. Two weeks into the war, he had the presence of mind to apply a tourniquet and to use a morphine syrette to mask his pain while he went about the job for which he had been trained.

War is hell for those on the front lines. It is also hell on loved ones at home.

—Sandy Cole

CHAPTER 7

Sandy Cole lives in her mother's small house on Aspen Street in Cadillac, Michigan. The tangible memories of her late husband—letters, photographs, medals—lie in a box in her home in Grand Rapids, 116 miles south, now occupied by a friend who is renting. She left in 2002, having taken an early retirement in 1996 from her office management job at the state veterans' home, to care for her aging mother and has not been back. She has family in the Cadillac area. Diagnosed with breast cancer in 2008, she managed to keep it from her mother even as she underwent surgery. Her mother died in 2009, on her 103rd birthday.[16]

Sandy was born on the family farm in the small town of Lucas, Michigan (population 1,500), the youngest of eight children, but after her parents' divorce, she went to live with her sister, Carol, and Carol's husband, John, in Grand Rapids. There she would meet her husband, Gordon Eugene Cole. They met as members of the choir of the Grand Rapids Central Seventh-day Adventist Church, an imposing building of rusticated red sandstone, built in 1894 for a Universalist congregation. Bought by the Adventists in 1939, it remains the city's principal Adventist church, now with a 350-seat sanctuary and embracing a number of Korean congregants.[17]

Gordon Cole was a tenor, a soloist with a "beautiful" voice, a voice framed by the church's 800-pipe Johnson Tracker organ. Gordon was born in the fall of 1943. His father worked for the telephone company, his mother for a local nursing home. He was close to her—a "mother's boy," in Sandy's words. He loved animals, and he loved cars. He owned a '63 black Corvair, "modified," according to his nephew, Larry Sluiter, for speed. He competed in local drag races and spent much time at car rallies and slot car races. Sandy went with him, recognizing, with good humor, that in those moments, his car and racing were his first love.[18]

They were married on 30 April 1967. Sandy remembers the exact time: 2:18 p.m. He was 23; she was a bit older. They were together for six months, living in an apartment in Grand Rapids, when the draft notice arrived. Sandy says that they both understood the meaning. Adventists were not to enlist, but if drafted, they were to serve as noncombatants, as COs.[19]

In the fall of 1967, Gordon Cole began his basic training at Fort Sam Houston. He would remain there for AIT (Advanced Individual Training) and would graduate 16 weeks later with an MOS (Military Occupational Specialty) of 91A—medical corpsman, and orders for Vietnam. He came home to Grand Rapids on leave. Most men came back from training far fitter and more muscular than they had been. Gordon, in Sandy's memory, came back like that, "tall, slender, handsome," taking her "breath away." He left for Vietnam in the late winter of 1968. It was the last time they saw each other.[20]

PFC Gordon Cole arrived in Vietnam on 8 March 1968, assigned to the 9th Infantry Division in the Mekong Delta. He did his job for five months or so and he had his orders, as Sandy remembers, for an R&R in Hawaii, in mid-August. They would meet there, as so many husbands and wives would. But something happened—orders were changed. Gordon stayed in Vietnam and died there—from multiple fragmentation wounds on 14 August 1968. Had his R&R orders not been changed, he and Sandy would have been together in Honolulu in that August week.[21]

Sandy was at work when the call came. Summoned home to her apartment, "upset, nervous, and in tears," she first learned that Gordon was "missing in action." The commandant of the veterans' home where she worked had dispatched a security guard to follow her to ensure she wouldn't be alone. Briefly relieved, she stayed home for a few days, anxious, waiting. It was better to work, she believed, and so she went back. Then a second call, a second visit, a week later. Gordon was dead. She remembers "falling on the couch in tears," but then gathering herself to go with the army officer to tell his mother, father, and brothers—"a hard and draining day . . . forever etched in my memory."[22]

The funeral was in Grand Rapids, at the Washington Park Cemetery. Sandy never viewed Gordon's body; one of his brothers advised against it. She now regrets it, feeling that she had "dishonored" him, though she understood she was still deeply in shock. She found the graveside service deeply moving—the crisp performance of the honor guard as they offered the customary three-volley salute, the presentation of the flag, "precisely . . . folded" and "creased," and then the "lonely" haunting sounds of "Taps." She remembers the Army escort, Sergeant Wright, staying beside her. Seven-year-old Larry Sluiter, Sandy's nephew, also remembered it, "vividly."[23]

Sandy never remarried. She fell away from her church. Her husband's death was part of the reason; so too were untrue ugly rumors that circulated in the church. In recent years, she has returned to the church, has been rebaptized, and volunteers at the local Adventist radio station—Strong Tower Radio. There is no bitterness in her voice. She can no longer embrace her husband, but her arms go out to all veterans and to the animals—dogs especially—that both she and Gordon loved. In her last message to me, she wrote that "she awaits to be reunited with Gordon in heaven when Jesus comes to take His believers home with Him."[24]

A Death at Mỹ Đồng

Gary Lee Abrahamson died in a night defensive position (NDP) near Mỹ Đồng on 20 September 1970 while serving as a medic. He was an Adventist and one of the last COs to die in Vietnam. He was born in Iowa in 1951 into a family of seven children, five boys, two girls. His father had joined an Adventist church when he was four. His oldest brother, Robert, born in 1937, followed his father into the faith. Drafted in 1960 as a CO willing to serve as a medic, Robert volunteered for Operation Whitecoat, the Army's program of medical experimentation, and served his two years at Fort Detrick. He remains deeply proud of his service, having attended the Whitecoat reunion in 2010.[25]

Gary attended Oak Park Academy in Nevada, Iowa, an Adventist high school since closed. There he met his future wife, Donita Bliss, who was born in 1951 on a farm in Cedar Rapids. They were engaged on graduation day in 1969. But Donita's parents were opposed. They thought her too young. Donita deeply respected her father, and so the engagement was broken. Gary responded by volunteering for the draft, meaning that he would be called up immediately, and so he was in the summer of 1969. Donita believes that the broken engagement prompted his decision.[26]

While Gary completed sixteen weeks of basic and medical training at Fort Sam Houston, Donita enrolled in an Adventist nursing school, affiliated with Hinsdale Hospital, in Chicago. Donita regretted her decision to break off the engagement. She told her parents that she had prayed about her marriage and was convinced that it was God's plan. And so she and Gary were married on 1 February 1970 in Cedar Rapids—he in his army uniform. They returned to live in an apartment in San Antonio. He had been assigned to hospital duty. It would not last. The need for medics in Vietnam remained overwhelming. He had his orders for Vietnam. Robert recalled a high-spirited departure dinner with Gary and Donita: "So much laughter," he said. Gary's father drove him to the airport that day and, on a different and discordant note, would confide to his granddaughter Karen that he did not believe Gary would return home.[27]

Arriving in-country on the 29th of June 1970, Abrahamson received his orders to report to Chu Lai in southern I Corps, once the home of the III Marine Amphibious Force, now the home of the Americal Division, a division whose memory will be forever tarnished by the massacre committed by its men two years earlier at My Lai. The Americal was a patchwork command reactivated only three years earlier, overseeing three brigades, two of which, the 11th and the 198th, had also been newly formed. Abrahamson had his orders for the 198th Light Infantry Brigade, and more specifically for the 5th Battalion of the 46th Infantry—the "Professionals."[28]

The 5th of the 46th was also a patchwork command, formed in the fall of 1967 at Fort Hood, Texas. They would train for Vietnam on the plains of West Texas using M14s. Their officers were fresh from the infantry school at Fort Benning; some of their older NCOs had served in Korea. Bravo Company initially had only one NCO with experience in Vietnam, but he, according to his company commander, was a "drunk" and a "loser." Some NCOs were clearly unfit for combat; others worked quickly to effect transfers. The young men who would bear the brunt of the war and would pay the highest price for the inexperience of their leaders were draftees or enlisted volunteers.[29]

In December 1967, the battalion learned that the president would review the troops, offer words of encouragement, perhaps share a meal in the mess hall with them. They waited in formation for an hour in the cold. When Lyndon Johnson finally appeared in an Army jeep, he passed in review without a glance, without a word, looking, according to one lieutenant,

CHAPTER 7

"ashen and . . . wrinkled . . . old beyond his years." The battalion commander sensed the anger and disappointment of his men.[30]

Training went on, and in early 1968 the battalion received an influx of 140 men, some of whom had failed Officer Candidate School (OCS); others had been reassigned prior to OCS training. Most of the latter were able to transfer out, but those who didn't posed serious morale problems. One young company commander, Kenneth W. McCarley, did his best to train his men for Vietnam, but recognized deeper problems. Having lost all confidence in the battalion's executive officer (second in command) and its operations officer, and after the battalion failed its first training test, he relinquished his command, an uncommonly principled act. The 5th of the 46th arrived in Vietnam at the end of March 1968. Four days later, Lyndon Johnson told the nation he would not run for president again.

The history of the 5th of the 46th in Vietnam will forever be linked to the writing of Tim O'Brien, whose first book, *If I Die in a Combat Zone*, recalled his service as a radio telephone operator (RTO) with an accuracy and verisimilitude largely lacking in his later and better-known works. O'Brien wrote convincingly of his respect for the competence and courage of his first company commander, and of the bravado and incompetence of his replacement—registering the ugly truth that the army had to recruit its junior officer class in the latter years of the war from a pool of men many of whom were unworthy of the responsibility.[31]

In March 1970, the battalion had been ordered to move from the dangerous coastal plain running from Chu Lai to Quảng Ngãi City, an area that included the village of My Lai, where the Army was still investigating the war crimes committed there two years previously. The battalion's new area of operations was in the mountainous regions west, south, and north of the division's base camp at Chu Lai. The brigade commander, Col. Joseph Clemons, of Pork Chop Hill fame, had made the decision, according to then Lt. Col. Norman H. Schwartzkopf, the commander of the battalion, because: "The Fifth of the Forty-sixth isn't cutting it down there. They're scared to death"—Schwartzkopf quoting Clemons. Schwartzkopf elaborated: "The troops had become so demoralized by the mines and booby traps that they'd lost their will to fight." But it wasn't just the 5th of the

46th, it was all of the 198th Brigade. Clemons again: "*I've* inherited the worst *brigade* in the United States Army" (italics in original). Fortune had not favored Gary Abrahamson.[32]

5/46's new Area of Operation (AO) offered no respite from mines and booby traps, made worse by a bad decision by an NCO new to the field to order his patrol down a recent tank trail, rather than cut a new, safer, trail. Sgt. Ronald Eugene Dills, 21, from Valparaiso, Indiana, died from a mine. Four others were wounded. Sp4 Shelton Ashworth lost his right arm and his right leg. "We cried throughout the night," Mike Laughlin remembered. Morale declined. In June, a young sergeant from C Company, 3rd Squad chose to set up a night ambush in the same position used a few nights earlier. An enemy platoon-size attack, initiated with grenades—they knew where they were—killed Sp4 David Concepcion-Nieves, from Arecibo, Puerto Rico, and wounded seven, including the medic, "Doc" Castillo. The rescuing squad found that a tripflare set to offer advance warning had malfunctioned, that 3rd Squad's Claymores had their wires cut, and ground radar units had detected movement just before the attack but there was "no system" in place to communicate with the squad.[33]

In early July, at the time Gary Abrahamson joined the battalion, Delta Company was patrolling in an area known as Dragon Valley in the midst of the Annamite Mountains northwest of Chu Lai. On 15 July, Delta took fire west of the Quan River from an NVA camp. They responded with mortars, then called in artillery and air support. They searched the camp after the enemy fled, discovering twenty-two structures, and two days later, three graves. On 28 July, they lost their Vietnamese Kit Carson scout, who mistakenly walked down the wrong trail and triggered an ambush with Claymores set previously by Delta. A booby trap grenade wounded two Delta troopers on 19 August. A few days later, the company destroyed two enemy bunkers, later wounded and captured a young VC, and hearing voices in a hooch near Long Sơn, a Delta trooper threw a grenade. A young woman suffered a head wound from the shrapnel. She and a boy beside her, who may or may not have been VC, were medevacked. Delta continued its patrols, uncovering a small enemy camp on 30 August, another on 5 September, while killing one NVA soldier two days earlier. There were further combat engagements on 12 and 19 September.[34]

The next day, after settling in for the night, Delta fired on several VC, spotted at 2130. Answering fire, from an unseen VC platoon "hidden in a tree line . . . two hundred yards east of Delta's perimeter," wounded one American in the shoulder. Another soldier broke down. At approximately 2140, the company called for dust-off. Sp4 Gary Abrahamson, tending to one of the two, was shot in the chest at approximately 2145. The first medevac mission failed, the helicopter crashing into trees on the perimeter of the landing zone at 2220. A second mission, at a second landing zone, arrived at 2330, picking up the four crew members of the first flight as well as other wounded—but they were too late for Gary Abrahamson. David Abrahamson, Gary's brother who was serving in Vietnam at the same time, accompanied his body home. David was not an Adventist and had chosen to enlist.[35]

Donita, who was pregnant, miscarried when she heard the news of her husband's death. She married again to a man who supported her desire to keep Gary's memory alive. When their house burned some years ago, according to his niece Karen Abrahamson, "the only thing that survived was a hope chest containing all the memorabilia from my uncle and his brief romance and marriage to my aunt."[36]

Four Medics

The late David Hackworth, a fierce and controversial combat officer, had an extraordinary respect for the medics who served under him: "They were the bravest of the brave . . . the most visible of the targets . . . [they] didn't wait for a miracle to pull the wounded out of a dangerous place—they provided the miracle." Hyperbole? Perhaps. Not every medic was a hero. And yet.[37]

Hackworth had a special respect for conscientious objector medics, and despite commanding more than 500 men, he remembered four of them by name. He also recalled that most medics who joined his battalion in 1969 were conscientious objectors. One was Billy Scott, who did not think he "was big enough or strong enough or brave enough to be a combat medic." Scott hid in the battalion chapel for two days when he first arrived, praying and fearful. The battalion surgeon finally drew him out and protected him for a time, keeping him at the aid station. But as platoon medics ended their tours they had to be replaced. Scott was assigned to a platoon whose former medic was a "big, rugged, profane" man who carried a weapon. His platoon mates, according to one, "weren't sure he could do the job ... [h]e was nervous and small and his medical aid bag was almost as big as he was." Yet he did his job, exposing himself to enemy fire to tend the wounded, an action that led to the award of a Bronze Star for Valor.[38]

When Billy Scott died of cancer in South Carolina at the age of 52, Hackworth wrote an obituary for this "warm, wonderful human being who'd cut his teeth on 'thou shalt not kill.'" Hackworth recalled the night of 13 March 1969 when Cpt. Eugene R. Spiegle [sic] died despite Scott's best efforts. Two other soldiers died that night, and nineteen were wounded. Scott was the only medic. To Hackworth he was "Little Billy," "one of the most courageous men I've known." "We loved his gentle ways, his lion heart, his total, selfless dedication to his soldier brothers."[39]

A second was Joe Cannon, from Queens. His platoon leader, Carl Ohlson, convinced him to carry a .45-caliber pistol, unloaded. "The VC don't care if you're a Quaker from Queens," Ohlson said, "[t]hey'll kill you in a heartbeat." Ohlson carried the loaded clips just in case. After a fire fight, Cannon gave the pistol back and requested an M16. "When these cats are shooting live bullets at me and they're flying over my head," he reportedly said, "my conscientious objector feelings disappear. I want to shoot back." Cannon later upgraded to an M79 grenade launcher. "He became one of the best shooters I ever had," Ohlson claimed.[40]

Another CO was Rick Hudson. His best friend was Nigel Frederick Poese, a radio telephone operator (RTO)—both were very religious. Poese had tripped a booby trap, and Hudson tried desperately to save him, to no avail. "A kid trying to save a kid," Hudson recalled, "and I couldn't save him. I'll never be able to get over that." Later hit in the leg and wrist from a round "that ricocheted off his rifle," he refused to be evacuated: "I'm the only medic." His platoon leader ordered him onto the helicopter.[41]

The fourth and last was Wally Nutt, who "gave his life while looking after his wounded ... buddies on a fire-swept field." Walter Lee Nutt III died in

CHAPTER 7

Vietnam on 28 March 1969 in the Mekong Delta, Kiến Phong Province. He was 22 years old, from Des Moines, Iowa.[42]

His picture graces the Virtual Vietnam Veterans Wall staring out at us in a graduation photo, a handsome, smiling young man in the era's narrow ties and lapels. The official army record of his death, date of birth, date of casualty, home of record, rank—a lowly PFC—offered no affirmation of his choice to serve as a CO.

For that you needed to have read Hackworth or understood the comments from Gary W. Rogers under the heading "Basic Training at Ft. Sam Houston." They were in the same class together, basic training for COs. Nutt was a squad leader, nicknamed "Tiny"—"He was a big guy and his voiced boomed whenever he spoke to his squad," Rogers remembered. In an email to me, Rogers would elaborate. "Every morning when our class was about to fall in to formation, we would hear Tiny bellow loudly. . . . 'Knock off that bullshit!' It became a ritual of our class." He had a "wonderful sense of humor" and everyone "knew that this command was delivered tongue in cheek." Rogers also remembered Tiny's "sense of duty to learn whatever needed to be learned" in army basic.[43]

Rogers was an Adventist and was accepted for Whitecoat duty. Nutt was not an Adventist. Rogers could not recall Nutt's faith community. Nutt had his orders for Vietnam. "I was sad to see Tiny and several other married guys getting orders for Nam. I had always believed that there was something horribly random about the way the Army decided where everybody was going to go." In his post on the Virtual Wall, Rogers also recalled that Tiny had a daughter and had a goal of going back to Des Moines to open his own restaurant.[44]

Then there was E. Gross, who also posted on the "Virtual Wall." Gross, who served with him, knew him as "Nutt," "a big man and a brave man of strong faith and good morals. . . . He told me that he wasn't going to carry a weapon. I worried about him but I respected and agreed with many of his reasons, and I knew that he was very sincere." Gross went on: "I have never forgotten him . . . he was such a fine human and I did have the good fortune to know him. . . . The price that Walter and many like him paid was not worth it."[45]

A third remembrance came from Dr. Byron Holley, his battalion surgeon. In a letter to his wife 1 June 1969, published in his book, *Vietnam, 1968–1969: A Battalion Surgeon's Journal*, Holley did not name the young medic killed, but it was almost certainly Walter Nutt: "One of my medics was killed last week. He was a hell of a fine kid, big handsome boy about 23, with a pretty wife and two sweet little children. He had been a conscientious objector (CO) when he first came to Nam but had not been here long before he had asked me to show him how to shoot a rifle, and I had gotten him an M16 of his own. I am very sad to learn of his death."[46]

The army awarded Wally Nutt the Distinguished Service Cross, posthumously. On a mission in Kiến Phong Province, his unit came under attack, the first two men in the patrol died, four more were wounded. According to the citation, "Private Nutt rushed through a hail of hostile fire and began to administer lifesaving aid to the injured. As he heroically made his way toward a third injured man, he was struck by enemy rounds which mortally wounded him. Private First Class Nutt's extraordinary heroism and devotion to duty, at the cost of his life, were in keeping with the highest traditions of the military service and reflect great credit upon himself, his unit, and the United States Army."[47]

CHAPTER 8

A Poet Returns from War

A week before Christmas, 1969, *The New York Review of Books* published "Poems from the Vietnam War." The author was Basil T. Paquet, a conscientious objector medic who had served in a hospital in Long Binh. His five poems were the first literary expressions of an antiwar veteran to appear in a nationally important publication, preceding by several years the better-known memoirs of Tim O'Brien (1973), Ron Kovic (1976), and Philip Caputo (1977).[1]

Two of the poems evoke stateside premonitions of injury and death of a sort common to all wars: "A Ride Home on His Final Leave" "stretches into blackness." The poet is "relieved at the darkness," as he writes of the "lie of youth, of my body—I am going to die." "Group Shot" contemplates a photo of a basic training class. "We are as once we were / The wholeness of our limbs / Two eyes blinking at the sun / When all had all needed/ to woo the world." A third poem brings us to the war. "Mourning the Death, By Hemorrhage, of a Child from Honai" opens with "Always the children are included / In these battles for the body politic." Honai, in the poet's note, is a village of North Vietnamese refugees near Long Binh known as "Sniper's Village." An American artillery attack would lead to "the mephitic / Stench of blasted bodies." The poet recognizes that "The enemy patriots knew the young / Would be glad to die for the revolution." Then "I could only wonder what ideology / The child carried in her left arm - necessity / Must have dictated an M16 round / Should cut it off, and her gaining the roll of martyrology."[2]

Another poem, "Morning - A Death," opens with the poet's effort to resuscitate a fallen soldier: "I've blown up your chest for thirty minutes /

And crushed it down an equal time, / And still you won't warm to my kisses." He continues employing the language of poetry as striking metaphors for his failed efforts: "I've scanned the rhythms of your living, / Forced half-rhymes in your silent pulse, / Sprung brief spondees in your lungs, / And the cesura's called mid-line, half-time, / Incomplete, but with a certain finality." The stanza closes with "You are dead just as finally / As your mucosity dries on my lips / In this morning sun. / I have thumped and blown into your kind too often / I grow tired of kissing the dead."[3]

Paquet would partner with two other veteran poets, Larry Rottmann and Jan Barry, to form 1st Casualty Press and publish the first anthology of poetry from the war, *Winning Hearts and Minds: War Poems by Vietnam Veterans*, in 1972. Barry was one of the co-founders of Vietnam Veterans Against the War (VVAW) and Rottmann and Paquet were both members. They sought "earnest artistic" work as well as pieces that "contributed to antiwar efforts." The anthology contains thirteen of Paquet's poems, the five from the *New York Review* (one slightly edited) and eight new ones. They are unrelievedly dark, poems of pain, death, and emasculation. The experience of failed resuscitation recurs. "Easter '68" ends with "only my breath on their lips, / only my words on their mouths." "It Is Monsoon at Last" contains the lines: "This dead boy is on my hands / My thighs are wet with the vomit of death / His blood is on my mouth / My mouth My mouth tastes his blood." "Basket Case" imagines an emasculated soldier, only recently having lost his virginity on "Tu Do Street" now with his legs blown off "fathering only this - the genderless bitterness / Of two stumps, and an unwanted pity." "They Do Not Go Gentle," with its allusion to Dylan Thomas, opens with an arresting simile: "The half-dead comatose / Paw the air like cats when they dream."[4]

Paquet chose not to write autobiographically—the persona of a poem is not necessarily the poet—"but through invented, composite fictional characters . . . crafted as vignettes or dioramic snapshots of the war." His aim was to capture "the horror, the evil, the damage, the contradictions, the chaos, the madness, and futility of that war as an agent of its happening." He chose to be there, "not a victim of the war, but a principal."[5]

Paquet's gifts as a poet were recognized by Stephen Spender in a review of *Hearts and Minds* in the *New York Review of Books*. Spender thought Paquet's poetry stood apart from the rest of the collection in its use of simile and metaphor and that Paquet had a "greater literary self-consciousness" and an "ambition which derives from an idea of poetry based on past experience and which exercises claims on the future." Spender had been a mentor to Paquet at the University of Connecticut and had facilitated the publication of his poems in the *New York Review*. Years later, a fellow veteran poet echoed Spender's praise: "Of the dozen or so poems Paquet contributes [to *Hearts and Minds*], three or four must rank as among the very best Vietnam war poems yet written" and that Paquet was then "far and away the most skilled and practiced of the soldier poets."[6]

The prominent New York publisher McGraw Hill took over responsibility for *Hearts and Minds*. The *New York Times, Newsweek, Hartford Courant, St. Louis Post-Dispatch, Chicago Sun-Times,* and *Philadelphia Sunday Bulletin* all reviewed it, and the book sold remarkably well for a collection of poetry. A year later, McGraw Hill brought out a collection of short stories by Vietnam veterans, *Free Fire Zone*, edited by Wayne Karlin, Larry Rottmann, and Basil Paquet. Paquet contributed one story. Joseph Pape staged a play in New York based on *Hearts and Minds*. Paquet's reputation in New York and nationally was further enhanced by his review of Mary McCarthy's *Medina*, a company commander at the My Lai massacre, in the *New York Review*. A third collection of poetry and fiction, *Postmortem,* edited by Karlin, Rottmann, and Paquet was in the works. McGraw Hill chose not to publish the work believing, according to Paquet, that another book on the war was no longer viable. Of course, the publishers were wrong, as the subsequent popular success of books by Ron Kovic, Philip Caputo, and others would demonstrate. Paquet and his co-editors closed 1st Casualty Press. Paquet, who was then married and teaching technical writing courses at the University of Hartford, went silent and would not publish poetry again.[7]

Paquet was born in East Hartford, Connecticut (working-class Hartford) in 1944 and lived initially in a government housing project built for workers

CHAPTER 8

and veterans. His mother was the child of Polish immigrants from Barre, Massachusetts. His father, born in Peterborough, New Hampshire (the model for Thornton Wilder's *Our Town*), came from French Canadian roots. He served in the Marines during World War II. He was a machinist who worked at Pratt & Whitney, a large manufacturer of aircraft engines, later founding his own company, Ourco Manufacturing, machining precision aircraft parts for the US defense industry.[8]

Paquet attended Catholic schools through his sophomore year and graduated from East Hartford High School in 1962. During summers he worked on the tobacco farms in the Connecticut Valley and continued to work—in warehouses, a steel mill, and a pharmacy—as he attended the Hartford branch of the University of Connecticut for two years. "There was not enough money for me to go away to college," he wrote in an email. He was, however, able to spend his last two years in Storrs, the university's main campus, majoring in English, reading Yeats, Randall Jarrell, Dylan Thomas, and the First World War poets Siegfried Sassoon and Wilfred Owen.[9]

His draft notice arrived during his senior year. He believed the American war in Vietnam was "immoral," that the US had replaced the French as a colonial power and were supporting a "puppet government" while standing in the way of forces "struggling to shake loose from the remnants of colonial rule." He recognized that Hồ Chí Minh's forces were supported by communist states but rejected the persisting anticommunist fears of the time (Vietnam was not Russia or China, he believed) as well as the "domino theory" that a communist victory in Vietnam would extend well beyond Vietnam. These were the conventional arguments of the antiwar movement, arguments he heard at teach-ins on the Storrs campus.[10]

He had to choose. At "great pain" to his family, he told his draft board that he would serve in uniform as a conscientious objector. He writes about his decision succinctly: "I believed in serving my country, was raised with that expectation (all my uncles were WWII vets) and thought that applying for CO status was a compromise I could live with or die for." My own experience was similar. My father, a prewar Marine and later an Army Air Corps bombardier, and his brother, a graduate of the Naval Academy and a submarine officer, were both veterans of World War II. Serving as a medic, rather than seeking alternative service, was a form of fealty to family and to country.[11]

Paquet was raised a Roman Catholic and remained so as he struggled over the draft. However, he sought no help from his church as he prepared his written request to serve as a CO medic. He claimed his decision was not religious, indeed that in 1966 he was the first "non-religious" CO in Connecticut. It may well have been true. The Supreme Court had only in 1965, in *United States v. Seeger*, broadened the definition of "religious training and belief" for those seeking CO status (see chapter 1 for the Seeger case). Yet in recent conversation, he implicitly qualified his definition of religion by noting that his decision emerged, if not from the tenets and practice of the Catholic Church, yet from a "Christian perspective" and from "Christian teaching."[12]

His draft board granted his CO exemption, and he reported to basic training in San Antonio in September 1966. Completing basic training and medical training, the latter of which he considered "terrific" because of the "army's ability to impart so much skill and knowledge" in such a short time, he fully expected to go to Vietnam. He went instead to Germany where he served for some months before volunteering to go to Vietnam. Arriving in the fall of 1967, the army assigned him initially to the 9th Infantry Division, likely for service as a line medic. However, he learned that he would be reassigned to the 24th Evacuation Hospital in Long Binh. He recalled being told that "any dumb ass fool could be a line medic," but that "we needed educated people like you for hospital work." It "likely saved my life," he wrote. The army did not routinely assign medics with college degrees to hospitals, but army personnel specialists did pay attention to education and test scores. At a much later point in the war, when the need for line medics had lessened, I experienced similar treatment as a college graduate who did well on standardized tests. Once assigned to a medical battalion, I never left the relative safety of the headquarters company.[13]

Paquet wrote that he worked "for a year in the pre-op and recovery section of the main neurosurgical hospital" serving all of South Vietnam, keeping people alive and "prepped" for surgery and then helping them recover: "Head and spinal trauma was the unit's specialization, but the severe trauma ran the gamut from amputations to penetrating wounds of the thorax and stomach." He treated "mostly severely wounded U.S. soldiers, but also enemy combatants, and civilian men, women, and children." He admitted, "The stress of being on duty was enormous, and I smoked and drank to excess off duty." After Tet '68, he developed a "stammer in my speech." His efforts to give mouth-to-mouth resuscitation, featured in his poetry, to a "dying, comatose soldier with encephalitis" led to his own case of encephalitis once he returned home.[14]

Home in September 1968: "Nobody cared or noticed," he wrote, "except my immediate family." His mom offered "typical" advice: "It's over now, and you can put it behind you and forget about it." He could not. "The war is something you cannot leave behind and is always with you—a part of your identity whether you want it or not," he wrote. He applied to the graduate school of the University of Connecticut for the second semester, worked as a substitute teacher, joined Vietnam Veterans Against the War (VVAW), and began writing poetry.[15]

He began his graduate studies in English in early 1969. He remembered it as "pure pleasure," mentored by Stephen Spender, taking classes with James Scully and Charles Olson. But he was far from a typical graduate student. He would soon be a nationally recognized antiwar poet, a writer for *The New York Review*, and, as mentioned, a founding member of 1st Casualty Press, with Larry Rottmann and Jan Barry, soliciting and editing poems and short stories for three volumes, two of which would be published by 1973. The work was consuming and would lead him to withdraw from graduate school. He also became active in VVAW, often meeting at Yale where William Sloane Coffin provided space.[16]

His involvement with VVAW proved fraught. He was arrested in Hartford after occupying a National Guard office. A protest against Spiro Agnew in New London led to the arrest of a VVAW "buddy." He took part in the large demonstration in Washington in the spring of 1971 (as did chapter three's David Rogers), which made John Kerry famous, and which riveted the nation as the nightly news captured veterans throwing their medals and ribbons onto the Capitol grounds, among them Paquet's Army Commendation Medal. "While marching in downtown DC," he recalled, being "attacked by cops," he "realized how easily things can turn a peaceful protest into something violent that would lead to more serious charges."[17]

In 1972 he left the country for Trinidad. He had married Sandra Pouchet, a Trinidadian whom he had met in graduate school. 1st Casualty Press was no more. Wayne Karlin had moved to Israel, Larry Rottmann to New Mexico. He had begun work on a novel and his wife was finishing her dissertation. He had a contract for the novel with Random House, but by the time he finished it his editor had moved on. He had a sense that the "window for writing about the war was closing." Of course, it wasn't, as Ron Kovic, Tim O'Brien, Philip Caputo, and Michael Herr would prove. But after McGraw Hill's decision to abandon "Postmortem," his belief was understandable. He was honest, however, in assessing his writing as an "artistic failure." The window for novels about the war "had closed for him."[18]

After some years living in the Caribbean, he and his wife returned to Hartford in 1977 to start a family, first one child and then twins. Sandra Pouchet Paquet finished her PhD in 1976. Both Basil and Sandra took university teaching jobs in Hartford. He taught technical writing courses. "We decided," he wrote, "we couldn't both teach and make it financially with three children we wanted to raise in circumstances far more comfortable than those in which we were raised." Among his students were insurance company staffers who advised him that he "could double or triple my income by joining the corporate world." And so he did, forging a "career in corporate training and organizational development." He "designed, developed, and taught corporate management and professional training courses." His wife, Sandra, established herself as a scholar of Caribbean literature and took up a professorship at the University of Miami. After moving to Florida, Basil Paquet served as a human resources executive for a number of companies. He is now retired.[19]

He never lost his interest in the war's literature. O'Brien's *The Things They Carried* "is rightly recognized as a great American novel." Herr's *Dispatches* captured "the absurd and tragic gestalt." He continued, "It was/

CHAPTER 8

is so difficult to capture the tone, tenor, and politics of the war and portray in proper balance the tragedy, horror, evil, and stupidity and absurdity of it all. How do you balance the bravery of the ordinary young men and women on all sides with the machinations of those who directed the war effort?" He believed that Karl Marlantes's novel *Matterhorn* comes closest to doing so. It reminded him of Norman Mailer's classic work, *The Naked and the Dead*, but Marlantes, he believed, "was more accomplished in marrying art and politics."[20]

He never lost his anger as well. Years after his service, in a fiery talk at the University of Miami, he spoke of it as a "war of attrition, oppression, even genocide," a war "against the Vietnamese people," "criminally" prosecuted. His judgments are harsh and misguided. Far too many Vietnamese civilians died as a result of the US's decision to wage battalion-level war in the countryside as well as its overreliance on artillery and aerial bombing, but this was not genocide, a globalizing word that can obscure the individual tragedies of unintended death. And, of course, this was not an American war against the Vietnamese people, but the continuation of a bloody civil war. The Viet Cong were not the Vietnamese people. But these were Paquet's judgments which, despite his service as a CO, implicated him, he believed, in the evils of the war.[21]

In that talk, Paquet recalled three incidents that exemplified for him the evils of the war and especially his own complicity in it. The first involved a chaplain priest's attempt to baptize a dying child in the absence of its mother. He called it a "spiritual kidnapping" and labeled the priest a "vulture" and a "jackal," harsh and overheated words perhaps explained by his decision to leave the Church after hearing a priest urging soldiers to "kill a commie for Christ." The second involved a stressed nurse beating the chest wound of a VC prisoner; the third a military intelligence (MI) officer telling a wounded 12-year-old boy, presumed to be VC whom Paquet was preparing for surgery, that he would be allowed to die unless he first gave information. Paquet intervened and spoke softly to the child. The boy spat at him, Paquet said, seeing "clearly what I don't want to see." "In the end," he continued, "there is no difference between the priest, the nurse, the MI, and me." Of course there was, a reasonable critic might say, but he could not see it, like David Rogers, so consuming was his guilt.²²

He has since begun to write again. He felt his work was "unfinished, and that I owed it to myself and my work to complete it." His typescript is titled "Group Shot," after one of his first poems, and comprises fifty-three poems, most written in 2022–2023, some previously published, a few of those recently edited. "Group Shot" is divided into two sections: "In Country" and "Back in the World," the "world" a common phrase of Vietnam veterans connoting home and suggesting Vietnam itself was not the known and familiar "world." The poet's persona has been enlarged. No longer just a hospital medic but an infantryman on patrol, "five days out, / Our squad stinks / So bad we know / The VC can smell us." ("Unfair Warning"). The poet knows "Friendly Fire," the drift of airborne herbicides ("Toxic Education"), and "Napalm," "modern warfare's / Vicious spin on Greek fire." Two of the poems, "Baby San" and "Bad Days," reprise his stories of the nurse, the priest, and the military intelligence officer.²³

Death remains a dominant theme. He comes to know, as so many veterans did, the fragility of the human body: "I believed my core / Was a solid oak trunk, and / War snapped it like a twig." The poem is "Expectant," the word signifying a soldier isolated in a hospital for whom there will be no further treatment. Reversing the hopeful meaning of the word, the soldier is expected to die. "Boatman" borrows the ancient metaphor for death's passage: "Holding the dying in your arms is hard. / You are the rope they grasp / Against the dark current / That pulls them under."²⁴

Guilt and complicity also remain. In "Johnny's Question," the poet makes clear to himself "That what you did in the war / Will haunt you all the days of your life, / And you will carry those memories to your grave." In "Weight of Stone," the poet seems to address another, or perhaps himself: "The long shame of his war years" will yield "the unbearable stench / Of his own unhealed corruptions." Language both harsh and unmeasured. Yet in a recent email, Paquet used, for him, the unexpected word closure, albeit in a qualified way. "I feel a sense of accomplishment in gaining closure," he wrote, "for the voices of those characters that speak in these poems [the poems of "Group Shot"]." "Of course," he continued, "closure is a funny word because war is not something you put behind you—it is there beside

CHAPTER 8

you for the rest of your life." "Beside you," not in you, perhaps no longer at the very core of your being. Am I reading too much into a single word?[25]

Some years ago I placed a cold call to a former Marine who had witnessed a war crime, reported it to a chaplain, and testified in a legal hearing preliminary to a court-martial. He didn't want to talk to me but I persisted. It seemed that he had never recovered from what he saw that day. He suffered from emphysema and would die within two years.

The day after our phone call we sang in church the beautiful Advent hymn "Comfort, Comfort, Now My People." I wrote to him in the next days and offered him the hymn's hope: "Tell them that their war is over." Would it be so for all those whose stories I've told and for all those who served.[26]

Epilogue

When I returned home from the Vietnam War in the spring of 1971, no one wanted to hear stories of heroism or self-sacrifice. The books that earned glowing reviews in the nation's liberal presses, and thus compelled the attention of readers, were memoirs of disillusion: Philip Caputo's *A Rumor of War*, Ron Kovic's *Born on the Fourth of July*, Lynda Van Devanter's *Home Before Morning*, among others. Michael Herr told his readers that the war was a surreal nightmare devoid of meaning. Tim O'Brien, as we've seen, wrote that stories of self-sacrifice, soldiers falling on grenades to protect their buddies, acts that have been extensively documented, were just trite bits of "puffery, pure Hollywood, untrue in the way that all such stories are untrue." And then there were the movies of the late 1970s, *The Deer Hunter* (1978), *Coming Home* (1978), *Apocalypse Now* (1979), reinforcing the pieties of all those who opposed the war. The disillusion of the war's veterans remains as riveting now as it did in the immediate aftermath of the war. Recall the extraordinary attention given to three such veterans—John Musgrave, Bill Ehrhart, Ron Ferruzzi—in Ken Burns's and Lynn Novick's *The Vietnam War*.[1]

Alongside the continuing appeal of disillusioned veterans, some of us have come to have a greater respect for those who served. In 1988, at the dedication of the Vietnam Veterans Memorial, President Ronald Reagan gave license to such respect when he referred to veterans as "champions of a noble cause." More recently, note the White House ceremonies for belated awards of the Medal of Honor, the ubiquitous, if also mawkish, "thank-yous for your service," directed at those Vietnam veterans wearing markers of such service. The Burns/Novick film also gave pride of place to the prominent veteran and author Karl Marlantes, who went to war despite his opposition to it. And, of course, so too did the thousands of men who served as conscientious objector medics opposed to killing in war.[2]

Yet it has taken far longer to honor such men. Why? One answer is simple misunderstanding. I've encountered people who had no idea that such service was possible. For them, COs were the ones doing alternative service. And yet there is another darker explanation. Years ago, I told my CO story to a short, smarmy fellow graduate student. His response suggested that I had been a sucker for serving. There were numerous ways to avoid service, he told me. I later learned that he had found one, overeating to the point where, too heavy for his height, he failed the physical. Recently, at a reception, I mentioned that I was writing about CO medics in the Vietnam War to a retired therapist, now a part-time musician. His immediate response: There should be a book about those who conned their way through draft physicals. The juxtaposition stunned me. Was a book about con men the appropriate rejoinder to a book about CO medics? He admitted that he had been such a con man, taking "bennies" to elevate his heart rate. He was unembarrassed. Many of his friends had done the same. Some of them may well have had questionable doctors' notes, just like Donald Trump, who we now know regards those who served and died as just so many "suckers."[3]

The largest obstacle to honoring the service of COs was, and remains, the nature of the war itself. It was immoral, I was told by my recent reception companion, a minority position during the time of the war but one that still lingers. Most Americans came to believe it was a futile failure, as it was. Sending infantry to fight a battalion-level war in the countryside, bombing a primitive country with a minimum of strategic targets, failing to halt the influx of arms from the North's communist allies as well as its troops coursing down the Ho Chi Minh trail, led where it must—unacceptable stalemate at best, loss at worst. Loss it was. After Nixon announced that the war would be "Vietnamized," every draftee with a brain understood that Nixon was admitting that the American war had been a mistake. Yet COs continued to raise their right hands.

They did so for different reasons. Some did so because their churches embraced the literal teachings of Jesus. Adventists did that and more, explicitly encouraging their sons to serve as unarmed medics. Others did so out of a sense of duty—but service on their moral terms. Some, such as David Rogers, because if they didn't someone else would take their place. Others came to weigh their moral options, deciding that noncombatant service was the best, and most authentic, choice out of all the bad, and morally questionable, options then available—the "greyness," as I've written, of an imperfect compromise. They did not leave their country. They did not con their way through draft physicals. They served. Their service, and on occasion their valor, has long been ignored. It should be no longer.

Notes

Introduction

1. The estimate derives from the work of Jean Anne Mansavage, "'A Sincere and Meaningful Belief': Legal Conscientious Objection During the Vietnam War" (PhD diss., Texas A&M University, 2000), 196–97. Neither the Selective Service System nor the Department of Defense kept records of noncombatant COs (1-A-0's as they were classified by Selective Service). Her estimate is based on the observation by the former commander of the US Army Medical Training Center that between 6 and 8 percent of those in medical training were COs. A second source, from the Central Committee for Conscientious Objection, offered the same percentage range.
2. George Q. Flynn, *The Draft: 1940–1973* (Lawrence: University Press of Kansas, 1993).
3. Mansavage, "A Sincere and Meaningful Belief," 196–97.
4. Ibid.
5. Gerald R. Gioglio, ed., *Days of Decision: An Oral History of Conscientious Objectors in the Military during the Vietnam War* (Trenton, NJ: Broken Rifle Press, 1989) contains oral histories of some CO medics, along with those who claimed CO status while in the military. James W. Tollefson, ed., *The Strength Not to Fight: Conscientious Objectors of the Vietnam War, In Their Own Words* (Washington, DC: Brassey's, 2000) contains interviews with alternative-service COs and those who fled to Canada, but the book is marred by its failure to name those interviewed. A selective sampling of books on Vietnam War dissent includes Charles DeBenedetti, *An American Ordeal: The Antiwar Movement of the Vietnam Era*

(Syracuse, NY: Syracuse University Press, 1990); Tom Wells, *The War Within: America's Battle Over Vietnam* (Berkeley: University of California Press, 1994); Nancy Zaroulis and Gerald Sullivan, *Who Spoke Up?: American Protest Against the War in Vietnam, 1963–1975* (New York: Doubleday, 1984); Stephen M. Kohn, *Jailed for Peace: The History of American Draft Law Violators, 1658–1985* (New York: Praeger, 1986); David Courtright, *Soldiers in Revolt: GI Resistance During the Vietnam War*, 2nd ed. (Chicago, IL: Haymarket Books, 2005); John Hagan, *Northern Passage: American Vietnam War Resisters in Canada* (Cambridge, MA: Harvard University Press, 2001).

6. See Gary Kulik, *"War Stories": False Atrocity Tales, Swift Boaters, and Winter Soldiers—What Really Happened in Vietnam* (Washington, DC: Potomac Books, 2009). The antiwar views of the 1960s linger in American scholarship: see Peter Zinoman, review of Mark Philip Bradley, *Vietnam at War* (New York: Oxford University Press, 2009) in H-Diplo/ISSF Roundtable II, no. 7, 2011. See also Kulik, review of Christian Appy, *American Reckoning: The Vietnam War and Our National Identity*, in "The War in Vietnam: Version 2.0," History News Network, 15 March 2015.

7. Dorothy Day, *The Long Loneliness: The Autobiography of the Legendary Catholic Social Activist* (New York: Harper & Row, 1952). Thomas Merton, *Raids on the Unspeakable* (New York: New Directions, 1964), read one New Year's Eve was especially important to me. Daniel Berrigan, *And the Risen Bread: Selected and New Poems* (New York: Fordham University Press, 1998). I wrote a paper on Berrigan's poetry my first semester in graduate school for an American poetry class. My effort to publish it was unsuccessful.

8. Fort Sam Houston Museum, *A Pocket Guide to Historic Fort Sam Houston* (San Antonio, TX: Fort Sam Houston Museum, 2004).

9. See Douglas Morgan, *Adventism and the American Republic: Public Involvement of Major Apocalyptic Movement* (Knoxville: University of Tennessee Press, 2001).

10. Tom Hirst's story is in chapter 4.

11. https://www.virtualwall.org/db/BennettTW02a.htm//; Bonni McKeown, *Peaceful Patriot: The Story of Tom Bennett* (Capon Springs, WV: Peaceful Patriot Press, 1987).
12. https://www.virtualwall.org/db/BrathwaiteRC01a.htm.
13. https://www.virtualwall.org/da/AbrahamsonGL01a.htm.
14. Kulik, "The War in Vietnam: Version 2.0."

Chapter 1

1. Peter Brock, *Pacifism in the United States: From the Colonial Era to the First World War* (Princeton: Princeton University Press, 1968), 10. The best summary of conscientious objection in America is John Whiteclay Chambers II, "Conscientious Objection and the American State from Colonial Times to the Present," in Charles C. Moskos and John Whiteclay Chambers II, eds., *The New Conscientious Objection: From Sacred to Secular Resistance* (New York: Oxford University Press, 1993), 23–46. In an otherwise admirable book, Adam Hochschild comes close to defining conscientious objection in "absolutist" terms focusing exclusively on those imprisoned for refusing noncombatant or alternative service. See his *American Midnight: The Great War, a Violent Peace, and Democracy's Forgotten Crisis* (New York: Mariner Books, 2002), 22, 144–48, 190–92, 287–88.
2. Brock, *Pacifism in the United States*, 10.
3. Ibid., 225.
4. Ibid., 159–81, 285–329.
5. Ibid., 199–200.
6. James Madison, "Proposals to the Congress for a Bill of Rights, 1789," in Lillian Schlissel, ed., *Conscience in America: A Documentary History of Conscientious Objection in America, 1757–1967* (New York: E. P. Dutton & Co, 1968); Richard Renner, "Conscientious Objection and the Federal Government, 1787–1792," *Military Affairs* 38, no. 4 (December 1974): 142–44.
7. John Whiteclay Chambers, II, *To Raise an Army: The Draft Comes to Modern America* (New York: The Free Press, 1987), 53. See also Ivor Bernstein, *The New York City Draft Riots: Their Significance*

8. Brock, *Pacifism in the United States*, 735; Schlissel, *Conscience in America*, 96, based on E. N. Wright, *Conscientious Objectors in the Civil War* (Cranbury, NJ: A. S. Barnes & Co, 1961), 72–73.
9. Schlissel, *Conscience in the United States*, 98. See also William C. Kashatus, *Abraham Lincoln, the Quakers, and the Civil War* (Santa Barbara, CA: Praeger, 2014).
10. Cyrus Pringle, *The Record of a Quaker Conscience, Cyrus Pringle's Diary* (Middletown, DE: n.p., reprint, 2020).
11. Ibid., 25, 32.
12. Ibid., 38.
13. Brock, *Pacifism in the United States*, 713, 737–38; Jacquelyn S. Nelson, *Indiana Quakers Confront the Civil War* (Indianapolis: Indiana Historical Society, 1991).
14. Brock, *Pacifism in the United States*, 823–61. The White quote is cited on 857.
15. Ibid., 843–44. See also Douglas Morgan, *Adventism and the American Republic: The Public Involvement of a Major Apocalyptic Movement* (Knoxville: University of Tennessee Press, 2001). On the lack of consensus among Adventist leaders, see Gilbert M. Valentine, *J. N. Andrews: Mission Pioneer, Evangelist, and Thought Leader* (Nampa, ID: Pacific Press, 2019), 285–90, 303–11 and Kevin M. Burton, "Seventh-Day Adventist Soldiers in the American Civil War and the Denominational Struggle for NonCombatant Recognition," in Jiri Moskala, et al., *Adventists, War, and Military Service: Biblical, Theological and Historical Perspectives* (Nampa, ID: Pacific Press (forthcoming)).
16. Francis McLellan Wilcox, *Seventh-Day Adventists in Time of War* (Takoma Park, DC: Review and Herald Publishing, 1936), 57–65; Arthur Whitfield Spalding, *Origin and History of Seventh-Day Adventists, Vol. 1* (Washington, DC: Review and Herald Publishing Association, 1961), 324. On evidence that Adventists took up arms, see Burton, "Seventh-Day Adventist Soldiers in the Civil War."

17. John Milton Cooper Jr., *Woodrow Wilson: A Biography* (New York: Alfred A. Knopf, 2009), 389, 393. See also Chambers, *To Raise an Army*, 205–37; David M. Kennedy, *Over Here: The First World War and American Society* (New York: Oxford University Press, 1980); Michael Kazin, *War Against War: The American Fight for Peace, 1914–1918* (New York: Simon & Schuster, 2017).
18. Chambers, *To Raise an Army*, 154.
19. Ibid., 173.
20. Schlissel, *Conscience in America*, 129–30; Chambers, *To Raise an Army*, 215–17.
21. Chambers, *To Raise an Army*, 216–17.
22. Kennedy, *Over Here*, 163; "Michael A. Stahl's Account" in John Stahl, ed., *Hutterite CO's in World War I* (Hawley, MN: Spring Prairie Printing, 1997), 9.
23. Chambers, *To Raise an Army*, 216; Norman Thomas, *The Conscientious Objector* (New York: B. W. Huebsch, 1923), 75; *New York Times*, 8 June 1917, 5; *Hartford Courant*, 3 November 1917; *Sacramento Union*, 29 September 1917; Harlan F. Stone, "The Conscientious Objector," *Columbia University Quarterly* 21, no. 4, (October 1919): 264; Frederick W. Keppel and Col. James S. Easby-Smith, *Statement Concerning the Treatment of Conscientious Objectors* (Washington, DC: GPO, 1919), 8.
24. Walter Guest Kellogg, *The Conscientious Objector* (New York: Boni and Liveright, 1919), 22, 131.
25. "Michael A. Stahl's Account," 15–16, 27–28; "Johannes Entz' Account," 18–19; "Jakob Waldner's Diary," all in *Hutterite CO's in World War I*. The latter was first published by Theron Schlabach, ed., "Diary of a Conscientious Objector," *The Mennonite Quarterly Review* 47 (January 1974): 73–111.
26. Kellogg, *The Conscientious Objector*, x; Sayre to Wilson, 27 April 1917, and reply, 1 May 1917, in Arthur Link, ed., *The Papers of Woodrow Wilson*, Vol. 42 (Princeton: Princeton University Press, 1983), 159–60, 179; *United States v. Seeger*, 165 in Schlissel, *Conscience in America*, 260–70.

27. Kellogg, *The Conscientious Objector*, 18–21; Wilcox, *Seventh-Day Adventists in Time of War*, 163–232.
28. Chambers, *To Raise an Army*, 216; *Sergeant York: His Own Life Story and War Diary*, ed. Tom Skeyhill (New York: Racehorse Publishing, 2018), 168–76; the York quote, 176.
29. Kellogg, *The Conscientious Objector*, 24, 99.
30. Ibid., 127.
31. Duane C. S. Stoltzfus, *Pacifists in Chains: The Persecution of Hutterites during the Great War* (Baltimore: Johns Hopkins University Press, 2013), 173–74; Schlissel, *Conscience in America*, 128–75; Louisa Thomas, *Conscience: Two Soldiers, Two Pacifists, One Family—A Test of Will and Faith in World War I* (New York: The Penguin Press, 2011), 102.
32. The Supreme Court upheld the constitutionality of the draft in *Arver et al., v. United States*, 7 January 1918. See Chambers, *To Raise an Army*, 219–20; Louisa Thomas, *Conscience*, 199, 213, 247–48.
33. Keppel and Easby-Smith, *Statement Concerning the Treatment of Conscientious Objectors*, 8; Norman Thomas, *The Conscientious Objector in America* (New York: B. W. Huebsch, 1923), 248.
34. Keppel and Easby-Smith, *Statement Concerning the Treatment of Conscientious Objectors*, 6–14; Norman Thomas, *The Conscientious Objector in America*, 289–92.
35. Wilcox, *Seventh-Day Adventists in Time of War*, frontispiece, 232.
36. Kellogg, *The Conscientious Objector*, 108–10; Stone, "The Conscientious Objector," 261; *Baltimore Sun*, 10 January 1919, 8; *Pittsburgh Press*, 13 November 1927, 26 and 6 May 1966, 41.
37. George Q. Flynn, *The Draft: 1940–1973* (Lawrence: University Press of Kansas, 1993), 45; Mulford Q. Sibley and Philip E. Jacob, *Conscription of Conscience: The American State and the Conscientious Objector, 1940–1947* (Ithaca, NY: Cornell University Press, 1952), 45–52.
38. Sibley and Jacob, *Conscription of Conscience*, 83, 69–71; Nicholas A. Krehbiel, *General Lewis B. Hershey and Conscientious Objection during World War II* (Columbia: University of Missouri Press, 2011), 145;

Stephan M. Kohn, *Jailed for Peace: The History of American Draft Law Violators, 1658-1985* (New York: Praeger, 1986), 47.

39. Krehbiel, *General Lewis B. Hershey*, 14–25. Hershey quoted in Flynn, *The Draft*, 46–47. See also George Q. Flynn, *Lewis B. Hershey: Mister Selective Service* (Chapel Hill: University of North Carolina Press, 1985).

40. Krehbiel, *General Lewis B. Hershey*, 100–118.

41. Ibid., 119–65; Flynn, *The Draft*, 47.

42. Sibley and Jacob, *Conscription of Conscience*, 91.

43. There are several biographies of Doss, among them Booton Herndon, *The Unlikeliest Hero: The Story of Desmond Doss, Conscientious Objector Who Won His Nation's Highest Military Award* (Mountain View, CA: Pacific Press Publishing Association, 2004); *Hacksaw Ridge*, 2016 film. More accurate is Terry Benedict's documentary *The Conscientious Objector*, 2004.

44. The Haynes quote comes from an interview in "Religion: Conscientious Cooperators," *Time*, 4 September 1950. See Sabrina Riley, "Medical Cadet Corps," 29 January 2020, encyclopedia.adventist.org. See also Roger G. Davis, "Conscientious Cooperators: The Seventh-day Adventists and Military Service, 1860–1945" (PhD diss., George Washington University, 1970).

45. Arthur W. Spalding, *Origin and History of Seventh-Day Adventists*, vol. 4 (Washington, DC: Review and Herald Publishing Association, 1962), 286–87, 292–95.

46. Leslie L. Coffin, *Lew Ayres: Hollywood's Conscientious Objector* (Jackson: University Press of Mississippi, 2012), 91.

47. Sibley and Jacob, *Conscription of Conscience*, 93–94.

48. See Flynn, *The Draft*, 88–109.

49. *Girouard v. US*, 328 US 61; Bill Galvin, "Conscientious Objection to the Korean War," *The Reporter for Conscience's Sake*, 76, Fall 2019, https://www.centeronconscience.org/files/Reporter_2019.pdf. See also Flynn, *The Draft*, 110–33.

50. On the opening of a dedicated basic training facility, see Mansavage, "'A Sincere and Meaningful Belief,'" 198. For a brief history of Operation

Whitecoat, see Bill Knott, "A Coat of Many Colors: Looking Back at Operation Whitecoat," *Adventist Review*, 24 September 1998, 8–13. See also Abel Rios, "Vietnam War and Seventh-Day Adventists," 10 May 2022, encyclopedia.adventist.org.

51. Department of the Army, Army Training Program, 21–111, *Modified Basic Training Program for Conscientious Objectors (1-Y-0) Without Prior Service*, 8 July 1964, U.S. Army Heritage and Education Center, Carlisle Barracks, PA.

52. Knott, "A Coat of Many Colors," is a fair-minded review. A harsh critique from within the church came from Martin D. Turner, "Project Whitecoat," *Spectrum: A Quarterly Journal of the Association of Adventist Forums* (Summer 1970): 55–70. Turner called on the church to renounce its support of "Project Whitecoat." Seymour Hersh, "Germ Warfare: For Alma Mater, God and Country," *Ramparts Magazine*, December 1969, 20–30.

53. See Knott, "A Coat of Many Colors." Jeffrey E. Stephenson and Arthur O. Anderson, "Ethical and Legal Dilemmas in Biodefense Research," in Borden Institute, *Textbook of Military Medicine* (Washington, DC, 2007) state that Operation Whitecoat was "a morally praiseworthy model for the conduct of biodefense research involving human subjects," 565; Phillip R. Pittman, et al., "An Assessment of Health Status among Medical Research Volunteers Who Served in the Project Whitecoat Program at Ft. Detrick, MD," *Military Medicine* 170, no. 3 (March 2005): 183–87.

54. "Operation Whitecoat," PBS, October 24, 2003. See also "Hidden History of U.S. Germ Testing," BBC, 13 February 2006. A robust defense of the program is the film by Randall Larsen and Aashish Edakadampil, *Operation Whitecoat, 1954–1973*, 2017.

55. Interview with Gary Rogers, 21 December 2016.

56. Mansavage, "'A Sincere and Meaningful Belief,'" 120; Schlissel, *Conscience in America*, 260–70; *Welsh v. United States*, 398 U.S. 333, 1970. By the 1970s, the percentage of Adventists claiming 1-A-0 status had declined to 35 percent to 40 percent, as more were seeking alternative service according to both the leadership of the church and

the Central Committee for Conscientious Objection; see Mansavage, "'A Sincere and Meaningful Belief,'" 120–21.

57. Kohn's evidence of a steep increase in objectors after 1970 is likely correct, but his measure of the percentage of objectors to inductees overstates the numbers of objectors by double or triple counting objectors as 1-Os, men affirmed for alternative service, 1-W, those serving in alternative assignments, and 4-W, those completing such assignments. See Mansavage, "'A Sincere and Meaningful Belief,'" 13, and notes 38, 39, 40, on pp. 24–25. In note 40, Mansavage cites the agreement of key Selective Service and Department of Justice officials that Kohn double or triple counted objectors.

58. The Department of Defense "Report to Congressional Requesters on Conscientious Objection," https://www.gao.gov/assets/gao-07-1196.pdf. The report suggested that there were likely more cases resolved at lower levels. Chambers, "Conscientious Objectors and the American State," 43–45 estimated 1,500 to 2,000. The activist lawyers Ronald Kuby and William M. Kunstler claimed that the numbers exceeded 2,500 in "Enduring the Storm: Conscientious Objectors in the Persian Gulf War," *St. John's Law Review* 66, no. 3 (Fall 1992): 655–86. The military required those applying as COs to deploy with their units. Those who refused or did not report faced court-martial charges. See Peter Applebome, "Epilogue to Gulf War: 25 Marines Face Prison," *New York Times*, 3 May 1991, 14. For the more recent wars, see GAO, "Military Personnel: Number of Formally Reported Applications for Conscientious Objection," 28 September 2007, in GAO-07-1196. See also Rowan Moore Gerety, "The Way of the Conscientious Objector," *New York Times*, 29 May 2021 and Larry Minear, "Conscience and Carnage in Afghanistan and Iraq: U.S. Veterans Ponder the Experience," *Journal of Military Ethics* 13, no. 2 (2014): 137–57.

Chapter 2

1. Lillian Schlissel, ed., *Conscience in America: A Documentary History of Conscientious Objection in America, 1757–1967* (New York:

E. P. Dutton & Co., 1968), 260, 263–64. See a recent publication of the memories of two more secular COs, James C. Kearney and William H. Clamurro, *Duty to Serve, Duty to Conscience: The Story of Two Conscientious Objector Combat Medics during the Vietnam War* (Denton: University of North Texas Press, 2023).
2. Interview with Dr. John Hubenthal conducted by Laura Calkins, Oral History Project of the Vietnam Archives, Texas Tech University, December 2005 to February 2006.
3. Information from the Vietnam Archives.
4. Interview with Hubenthal, 102, 17.
5. David J. Morris, *The Evil Hours: A Biography of Post-Traumatic Stress Disorder* (New York: Houghton Mifflin Harcourt, 2015), 44.
6. Interview with Hubenthal, 66.
7. Ibid., 134. Michael Sallah and Mitch Weiss, *Tiger Force: A True Story of Men and War* (New York: Little, Brown and Company, 2006); see the many references to Sam Ybarra.
8. Interview; obituary, *Boston Globe*, 6 September 2006.
9. Interview, 17.
10. Interview, 105; Kurt Vonnegut, *Slaughterhouse-Five* (New York: Delacorte, 1969).
11. Richard J. McNally, "The Things They Carry Home," *Wall Street Journal*, 13 February 2015. See also Richard J. McNally, *Remembering Trauma* (Cambridge: Harvard University Press, 2003); Allan Young, *The Harmony of Illusions: Inventing Post-Traumatic Stress Disorder* (Princeton: Princeton University Press, 1995), 6; and Gary Kulik, *War Stories: False Atrocity Tales, Swift Boaters, and Winter Soldiers* (Washington DC: Potomac Books, 2009), 41–51.
12. Richard A. Kulka, et al., *Trauma and the Vietnam War Generation: Report of Findings from the National Vietnam Veterans Readjustment Study* (New York: Brunner/Mazel, 1990), 130, 223ff; Bruce P. Dohrenwend, et al., "The Psychological Risks of Vietnam for U.S. Veterans: A Revisit with New Data and Methods," *Science*, 313, August 18, 2006, 979–82. See also Richard J. McNally, "Revisiting Dohrenwend, et al., Revisit of the National Vietnam Veterans

Readjustment Study," *Journal of Traumatic Stress* 20, no. 4 (August 2007): 481–86. On the study of resilience, see George A. Bonanno, *The End of Trauma: How the New Study of Resilience Is Changing How We Think about PTSD* (New York: Basic Books, 2021).

13. Interview, 6.
14. Ibid., 19.
15. Ibid., 24.
16. Ibid., 25.
17. Obituary, comment by Charles Heard.
18. Interview, 35.
19. Ibid., 42.
20. Ibid., 42.
21. Ibid., 53
22. Ibid., 61.
23. Ibid., 56.
24. Ibid. Hubenthal was neither the first nor the last who would regard the Whitecoat program as sinister, but he missed the core of its meaning. This was a program open only to Seventh-day Adventists (SDAs), none of whom were "snake-handlers." See chapter 1 for a discussion of the Whitecoat program.
25. Ibid., 71, 73.
26. Ibid., 70.
27. For a critique of the failure of the army to train men for the war in Vietnam, see Col. David H. Hackworth and Julie Sherman, *About Face* (New York: Simon & Schuster, 1989), 625–45.
28. Interview, 96–97.
29. Ibid., 97.
30. Ibid., 93–95.
31. Ibid., 97.
32. Ibid., 99–100.
33. Ibid., 118.
34. Ibid.
35. Ibid., 129.
36. Ibid., 130.

37. Ibid., 134.
38. Hackworth and Sherman, *About Face*, 485.
39. Sallah and Weiss, *Tiger Force*.
40. Ibid., 11–12, 62–63, 128, 197–98, 200, 202, 203, 208–9, 211, 212–14, 255, 265, 274, 302–3, 330, 335, 346, 360–61, 363–64, 371, 372–74, 383.
41. Interview, 135.
42. Ibid., 32, 36.

Chapter 3

1. David Rogers, interviewed by James P. Sterba, "Close-up of the Grunt," *New York Times*, 8 February 1970. I found my way to Rogers through the good offices of the late James Wright, who interviewed him for his *Enduring Vietnam: An American Generation and its War* (New York: St. Martin's Press, 2017). Max Hastings also interviewed Rogers for his *Vietnam: An Epic Tragedy, 1945–1975* (New York: HarperCollins, 2018).
2. Sterba, "Close-up of the Grunt."
3. Ibid.
4. Interview, 31 July 2017.
5. Interview; David Rogers, C-SPAN.org, 13 January 1994.
6. Email, David Rogers to author, 21 July 2017.
7. Interview.
8. Interview; TheWall-USA.com, Wayne Russell. Russell served as a medic in the 1st Cavalry Division. He was killed 31 March 1969. On the "Black Lions," see David Maraniss, *They Marched into Sunlight: War and Peace, Vietnam and America, October, 1967* (New York: Simon & Schuster, 2003). On casualty rates by month, see AmericanWarLibrary.com/vietnam.
9. Email, Rogers to author, 2 August 2017.
10. Rogers wrote about Richard in "Trump's Vietnam Draft Past Sheds Light on 'Sacrifice' Debate," *Politico*, 1 August 2016. "When Donald Trump talks about his 'sacrifices,' I think of Richard from Trump's own Queens, New York, who was killed in my infantry company

in Vietnam in 1969." Rogers did not want me to use Richard's last name in deference to Green's family. But I found my way to other sources that identified him. See Peter P. Joyce Jr., "Serving in Vietnam with Richard Hershel Green," at https://www.mainememory.net/sitebuilder/site/2655/page/4263/display and https://www.vvmf.org/Wall-of-Faces/19813/RICHARD-H-GREEN/.

11. Email, Rogers to author, 2 August 2017; Wall of Faces/32431/Ellis-S-Marlin.
12. Interview.
13. Interview; email from Rogers to author, 21 July 2017.
14. Interview.
15. Interview, David Rogers, C-SPAN.org, op. cit. and https://www.adweek.com/performance-marketing/politico-welcomes-david-rogers/.
16. Interview, 18 January 2008.
17. Shorensteincenter.org/mark-halperin, 20 October 2014; Dylan Byers, "Kerry Thanks Reporters, *Politico*'s Rogers," *Politico*, 30 January 2013.
18. Mariness, *They Marched into Sunlight*; David Rogers, "TV Cameras Gone, the Grief Is Private," *Boston Globe*, 12 November 1982, 3.
19. Rogers, "TV Cameras Gone"; interview.
20. Rogers, "TV Cameras Gone."
21. Interview; David Rogers, "Bouncing Back: Brick Houses and Soda on Ice Bear Witness to Vietnam's Revival," *Wall Street Journal*, 6 January 1994, A1.
22. David Rogers, C-Span.org; interview; Rogers, "Bouncing Back."
23. Rogers, C-Span.org.
24. The best recent history of North Vietnam is Christopher Goscha, *The Road to Dien Bien Phu: A History of the First War for Vietnam* (Princeton: Princeton University Press, 2022). On "Doi Moi," see William S. Turley and Mark Selden, *Reinventing Vietnamese Socialism: Doi Moi in Comparative Perspective* (London: Routledge, 1993).
25. Trump quoted in Rogers, "Trump Evades Specifics on his Draft Deferment," *Politico*, 19 July 2015.

26. Ibid.
27. Rogers, "Trump's Vietnam Draft Past."
28. Ibid.
29. Interview.
30. Interview.

Chapter 4

1. Roger Guion Davis, "Conscientious Cooperators: The Seventh-day Adventists and Military Service, 1960–1945," PhD diss., George Washington University, 1970.
2. http://army.togetherweserved.com/army/voices/2013/66/Hirst_voices.html, hereafter, Hirst, "together we served." There is also a Tom Hirst YouTube page covering the same ground. Additional biographical information on Hirst comes from an email from Hirst to the author, 26 February 2022.
3. Hirst, email to author, 30 November 2017.
4. Ibid.
5. *Takoma Academy Yearbook*, 1967 in the possession of Karen Sewell.
6. Ibid. Phone interview with Tom Hirst, 29 August 2017.
7. Phone interview with Terry Sewell, 9 June 2017 followed by a face-to-face interview, 27 September 2017.
8. *Blue Mountain Academy Yearbook*, 1967, in the possession of Karen Sewell.
9. Phone interview with Tom Hirst.
10. Ibid.; Hirst, "together we served."
11. Phone interview with William Hall, 5 September 2017; https://www.vvmf.org/Wall-of-Faces/7285/NOLAN-D-BYRD/.
12. Phone interview with William Hall.
13. Ibid.
14. Ibid.; interview with Tom Hirst.
15. Phone interview with William Hall, 5 September 2017.
16. Phone interview with William Hall.
17. *Takoma Academy Yearbook*, 1969.
18. Interview with Terry Sewell, 27 September 2017.

NOTES

19. Interview with Tom Hirst.
20. Hirst, "together we served."
21. Ibid.
22. Ibid.
23. Michael B. Christy, "Smashing Sanctuaries in Cambodia," *Vietnam* 23, no. 2, August 2010, 24; Hirst, "together we served."
24. Christy, "Smashing Sanctuaries," 24–25.
25. Ibid., 25.
26. Hirst, "together we served."
27. Ibid.
28. Ibid.
29. Ibid. Christy, "Smashing Sanctuaries," 25.
30. Hirst, "together we served."
31. Ibid.
32. Ibid.
33. Christy, "Smashing Sanctuaries," 29.
34. Hirst, "together we served."
35. Interviews with Tom Hirst and Terry Sewell. https://www.vvmf.org/Wall-of-Faces/13330/JAY-T-DILLER/. The attack on FSB Henderson is recounted in Keith W. Nolan, *Ripcord: Screaming Eagles Under Siege, Vietnam 1970* (Novato, CA: Presidio Press), 91–92. See also George Banda, "My War," www.wisconsinstories.org/vietnam. Banda served with Diller. Another account is Charles F. Hawkins, "Hell Night at Henderson," *VFW Magazine*, August 2010, 28–30.
36. Nolan, *Ripcord*, 91–92.
37. Ibid, 91.
38. Ibid., 92.
39. Ibid., 92; Banda, "My War."
40. Ray Wenger's comments appear on the Wall of Faces/JAY-T-DILLER.
41. Hirst, "together we served."
42. Interview with William Hall. William E. Hall Sr., died on 28 August 2024. See https://www.youtube.com/watch?v=1xoBCyc6_S8&ab_channel=WPSDAMediaMinistry.

43. Email from Karen Sewell to the author, 27 February 2022.

Chapter 5

1. John T. Wheeler, "War Hating Miamian Is a War Hero"; Ian Gross, "He Is a Gentle GI Who Reads the Bible Every Day," *Miami News*, 11 March 1968.
2. Ray Stubbe's account is based on four sources. The first, drawing upon his diary, is his *Battalion of Kings: A Tribute to Our Fallen Brothers Who Died Because of the Battlefield of Khe Sanh, Vietnam*, 2nd ed. (Wauwatosa, WI: Khe Sanh Veterans, Inc., 2008), 253–55. The second is an oral history interview with Rev. Ray W. Stubbe, 2005–2006, by the Wisconsin Veterans Museum Research Center, 15–18 at https://wisvetsmuseum.com/ohms-viewer/render.php?cachefile=OH_01324.xml. The third is a more recent interview of Stubbe, 8 August 2018 to be found on vimeo.com/284074204. The fourth is an interview with the author, 9 September 2018.
3. Stubbe, 2005–2006 oral history interview, 17–18; Stubbe, *Battalion of Kings*, 253.
4. Letter of George Anderson to Dennis Smith, 11 February 1991, quoted in Stubbe, *Battalion of Kings*, 253.
5. Letter of Earl Clark, 4 March 1969, in Khe Sanh Veterans, *Red Clay* 46 (Spring 2000), quoted in Stubbe, *Battalion of Kings*, 253–54.
6. Stubbe, 2005–2006 oral history interview. Telephone interview with the author, 9 September 2018. An additional oral history interview with Stubbe is in Ron Steinman, ed., *The Soldiers' Story: Vietnam in Their Own Words* (New York: Fall River Press, 2011), 65–70. See also Michael E. Ruane, "This Brave Ex-Chaplain Is Still Haunted by the Vietnam War's Most Desperate Siege," *Washington Post*, 22 January 2018.
7. Stubbe, 2005–2006 oral history interview, 15; 2018 interview with author.
8. Stubbe, 2005–2006 oral history interview, 16.
9. Ibid.
10. Ibid.

11. Ibid.
12. In addition to his two editions of *Battalion of Kings*, Stubbe co-authored with John Prados, *Valley of Decision: The Siege of Khe Sanh* (New York: Houghton Mifflin, 1991); interview with author, Vimeo interview.
13. Interview with author.
14. Ibid., 2005–2006 interview, 18, Dan Sullivan email to author, Jan K. Herman, ed., *Navy Medicine in Vietnam: Oral Histories from Dien Bien Phu to the Fall of Saigon* (Jefferson, NC: McFarland & Company, 2009), 249. See also James O. Finnigan, *In the Company of Marines: A Surgeon Remembers Vietnam* (Middletown, DE: Lulu.com, 2009), 97–101.
15. Herman, *Navy Medicine*, 249–50.
16. Ibid., 250.
17. John Randolph, "Those Jungle Boots Echo from Khe Sanh," *Los Angeles Times*, 18 March 1968, 5. The story was widely reported at the time with versions appearing in newspapers in Miami, Cincinnati, Rochester, Asheville, Phoenix, and Baltimore, among other places. See Newpapers.Com for the full list.
18. Jurate Kazickas, "Those Hills Called Khe Sanh," in Tad Bartimus, et al., *War Torn: Stories of War from the Women Reporters Who Covered Vietnam* (New York: Random House, 2002), 120–53.
19. Ibid., 145–46.
20. Randolph, "Those Jungle Boots Echo . . ."
21. The language of Spicer's Navy Cross can be found on https://www.vvmf.org/Wall-of-Faces/49166/JONATHAN-N-SPICER/. Both Stubbe and Dan Sullivan remember the wounding of Spicer differently from the Navy Cross citation. Sullivan specifically recalled that an artillery round hit Charlie Med, killing three and wounding as many as twenty.
22. https://en.wikipedia.org/wiki/James_Anderson_Jr. and Larry_G._Dahl.
23. Richard E. Killblane, *Circle the Wagons: The History of US Army Convoy Security* (Ft. Leavenworth, KS: Combat Studies Institute,

2012), Kindle ed., 57–58.
24. Émile Durkheim, *Suicide: A Study in Sociology* (New York: The Free Press, 1951), 234.
25. Durkheim, *Suicide*, 239–40; Joseph A. Blake, "Death by Hand Grenade: Altruistic Suicide in Combat," *Suicide and Life-Threatening Behavior* (Spring 1978); Jeffrey W. Riemer, "Durkheim's 'Heroic Suicide' in Military Combat," *Armed Forces & Society* 25, no. 1 (Fall 1998), 103–20.
26. Kazickas, "Those Hills Called Khe Sanh," 136.
27. Joseph Galloway, "Besieged Soldier Didn't Think He Would Make It," *The Town Talk*, Alexandria, Louisiana, 23 February 1971, 18. "Isle GI Stays with Viet Rangers," *Honolulu Advertiser*, 22 February 1971, 1; "Fujii Due for Hero's Welcome," *Honolulu Star-Bulletin*, 28 February 1971, 1. Fujii's Distinguished Service Cross Citation can be found at https://valor.militarytimes.com/hero/4580. See also Keith Nolan, *Into Laos: The Story of Dewey Canyon II/Lam Son 719I* (Novato, CA: Presidio Press, 1986), 128–30, 134–37 and Karen Blakeman, "Hero from Hawai'i Lands in Aviation Hall of Fame," https://the.honoluluadvertiser.com/article/2004/May/10/mn/mn01a.html. Fujii's Medal of Honor citation can be found at https://www.army.mil/medalofhonor/fujii/.
28. Tim O'Brien, *The Things They Carried* (Boston: Houghton Mifflin, 1990), 89. Michael Herr, *Dispatches* (New York: Alfred A. Knopf, 1968). For a critique of Herr and O'Brien, see my *"War Stories": False Atrocity Tales, Swift Boaters, and Winter Soldiers* (Washington, DC: Potomac Books, 2009), 26–33.
29. O'Brien, *The Things They Carried*, 89–90.
30. Ibid., 76; Ernest Hemingway, *A Farewell to Arms* (New York: Macmillan, 1986), 184; Paul Fussell, *Wartime: Understanding and Behavior in the Second World War* (New York: Oxford, 1989), ix, 132.
31. Fussell, *Wartime*, 296, 292; O'Brien, *If I Die in a Combat Zone, Box Me Up and Ship Me Home* (New York: Laurel, 1987).
32. Stubbe, interview with author; Wheeler, "War Hating Miamian is

a War Hero," "Unwilling Hero Dies of War Wounds," *Louisville Courier Journal*, 15 March 1968, 8.

Chapter 6

1. Ron Donahey, *Vietnam Combat Medic: A Conscientious Objector in the Central Highlands* (Athens, GA: Deeds Publishing, 2019); Clifford S. Roberson, *Vietnam Medic: Field Journal* (Ukiah, CA: CaeSaR Books, 2011); C. Michael Dingman, *Unlikely Warrior: Memoirs of a Vietnam Combat Medic* (Zulon Press, 2014).
2. Donahey, *Vietnam Combat Medic*, ix.
3. Donahey, https://www.youtube.com/watch?v=G7uizc_rAjM&ab_channel=VictorPhillips; Donahey, *Vietnam Combat Medic*, 3.
4. Roberson, *Vietnam Medic*, 10; Dingman, *Unlikely Warrior*, 37.
5. Donahey, YouTube interview; interview with author, 3 April 2022.
6. Donahey, *Vietnam Combat Medic*, 8.
7. Dingman, *Unlikely Warrior*, 42. Dingman and I were in basic training at the same time, in the summer of 1969. We were, however, in different classes and did not know each other. Each class occupied a different part of the Long Barracks and did not train together.
8. Ibid., 45; Gary Kulik, *"War Stories": False Atrocity Tales, Swift Boaters, and Winter Soldiers—What Really Happened in Vietnam* (Washington: Potomac Books, 2009), 5–7.
9. Roberson, *Vietnam Medic*, 20–21, 19.
10. Ibid., 25, 26.
11. Donahey, *Vietnam Combat Medic*, photo on 23; Herbert Ford, *No Guns on Their Shoulders* (Nashville: Southern Publishing Association, 1968), 110, 111.
12. Philip Caputo, *A Rumor of War* (New York: Henry Holt and Company, 1977), 66; Lt. Gen. Harold G. Moore (Ret.) and Joseph L. Galloway, *We Were Soldiers Once…And Young* (New York: Random House, 1992).
13. Dingman, *Unlikely Warrior*, 50; Roberson, *Vietnam Medic*, 28; Donahey, *Vietnam Combat Medic*, 39, 63, 29, 30. The betel nut is a cancerous stimulant that turns teeth and lips a dark red. Montagnard

is a French term for some thirty Indigenous tribes in the Central Highlands comprising six different ethnic groups who mostly fought on the side of Americans. Also known as Degars, many converted to Christianity and now their largest settlement in the world is in Greensboro, NC. See Gerald Hickey, *Shattered World: Adaptation and Survival among Vietnam's Highland People during the Vietnam War* (Philadelphia: University of Pennsylvania Press, 1993).

14. Donahey, *Vietnam Combat Medic*, 27, 69.
15. Roberson, *Vietnam Medic*, 82, 87; Dingman, *Unlikely Warrior*, 96, 111.
16. Roberson, *Vietnam Medic*, 35.
17. Donahey, *Vietnam Combat Medic*, 72.
18. Ibid., 78–79.
19. Ibid., 149.
20. Ibid., vii; https://www.vvmf.org/Wall-of-Faces/18638/WILLIAM-A-GILMORE-2/.
21. Donahey, *Vietnam Combat Medic*, 56, 161.
22. Ibid., 166, 138; interview with author.
23. Roberson, *Vietnam Medic*, 66, 70; https://www.vvmf.org/Wall-of-Faces/52965/WILLIE-TYLER/.
24. Roberson, *Vietnam Medic*, 97.
25. Ibid., 123, 130; https://www.vvmf.org/Wall-of-Faces/43149/ANTONIO-RIBERA/.
26. Roberson, *Vietnam Medic*, 181; https://www.vvmf.org/Wall-of-Faces/18334/HOWARD-M-GERSTEL/ and https://www.vvmf.org/Wall-of-Faces/46124/DONALD-G-SCHRENK/page/2/. On Together We Served, Schrenk, Donald George, Roberson posted a message referring to Schrenk as a "fellow SDA."
27. Roberson, *Vietnam Medic*, 113, 107. On the myth of prisoners thrown from helicopters, see my *"War Stories,"* 131–38.
28. https://www.vvmf.org/Wall-of-Faces/17769/BENJAMIN-GARCIA/. Dingman posted on the site, "You died trying to save another man's life and the bullet that took yours could have just as easily taken mine."

29. https://www.vvmf.org/Wall-of-Faces/45326/VICTOR-S-NICOLAS/ and https://www.vvmf.org/Wall-of-Faces/49187/GEORGE-T-SPILLERS/. On the medevac missions, Dingman relied on operational reports for the 3rd Battalion, 506th Infantry.
30. Dingman, *Unlikely Warrior*, 94, 95.
31. Quoted in ibid., 142.
32. Donahey, *Vietnam Combat Medic*, 186.
33. Donahey, interview with author.
34. Ibid., Donahey, YouTube interview.
35. Roberson, *Vietnam Medic*, 227, 231.
36. Ibid., 232, 225.
37. Ibid., 237, 247–70.
38. Ibid., 243.
39. See Mike Dingman's LinkedIn page.
40. Dingman, *Vietnam Combat Medic*, 272–73; email, Dingman to author, 28 March 2020.
41. Email, Dingman to author.

Chapter 7

1. Randy K. Mills, *Troubled Hero: A Medal of Honor, Vietnam, and the War at Home* (Bloomington: Indiana University Press, 2006), 86.
2. Keith W. Nolan, *Ripcord: Screaming Eagles Under Siege, Vietnam 1970* (Novato, CA: Presidio, 2000), 93–94. A more detailed account can be found in Mills, *Troubled Hero*, 80–114. The quote from his friend is in Mills, *Troubled Hero*, 109. For the citation, see cmohs.org/recipients/kenneth-m-kays.
3. Mills, *Troubled Hero*, 14, 15, 16, 17, 21.
4. Ibid., 28–37. The Thompson quote is from the *Wayne County Press*, 3 November 1969, cited in Mills, 35. The drug use quote is cited in Mills, 35.
5. The David Steiner article appeared in the *Wayne County Press*, 21 August 1969, cited in Mills, *Troubled Hero*, 44. "Fairfield Boy" appeared in the *Press*, 1 September 1969, cited in Mills, 45. See also Mills, 38–47.

6. Mills, *Troubled Hero*, 30, 48–53, 14.
7. Ibid., 48–55. The quoted passages are on 54. Mills speculates that he would have been treated harshly as a CO in basic training, but there is no evidence for this, and he wasn't a recognized CO. To complete basic training, he would have had to qualify on the rifle range.
8. Ibid., 111, 115.
9. Ibid., 115. The quote comes from the *Wayne County Press*, 7 January 1971, in ibid., 116. The poem comes from a portion of Kays's personal journal, cited in ibid., 116–17.
10. Ibid., 114–20. The quotes appear on 118, 120, 119.
11. Ibid., 120–24. The quotes come from the *Wayne County Press*, 3 June 1974, cited in Mills, 122. "Long sun-tented hair" comes from the *Sedalia Democrat*, 13 June 1974, cited in Mills, 123.
12. Mills, *Troubled Hero*, 126. The quote from Kays comes from Edward F. Murphy, *Vietnam Medal of Honor Heroes* (New York: Ballantine Books, 1987), 252.
13. A. James Liska, "Kenny Kays's Saga," *The Daily Illini*, 8 May 1976, 24–25.
14. Mills, *Troubled Hero*, 126–28.
15. Ibid., 129–31. Mills had access to Kays's journal, but he provides no specific reference to the quote suggesting that his father kill himself.
16. Interviews with Sandy Cole, 25 and 26 October 2012, 21 November 2012. An excellent book on the travail of Vietnam War widows is Andrew Wiest's *Charlie Company's Journey Home: The Forgotten Impact on the Wives of Vietnam Veterans* (Oxford, UK: Osprey Publishing, 2018). It is a sequel to his *The Boys of '67: Charlie Company's War in Vietnam* (Oxford, UK: Osprey Publishing, 2012). The latter book tells the story of Gary Maibach, a CO medic. The former introduces his wife, Mary Ann Maibach.
17. Ibid.
18. Ibid.; interviews with Larry Sluiter, 4 and 10 October 2012.
19. Interviews with Sandy Cole.
20. Ibid.
21. The Virtual Wall, GORDON EUGENE COLE; https://www.vvmf.

org/Wall-of-Faces/9742/GORDON-E-COLE/.
22. Interviews with Sandy Cole.
23. Ibid.; interviews with Larry Sluiter.
24. Interview with Sandy Cole.
25. https://www.virtualwall.org/da/AbrahamsonGL01a.htm; https://www.vvmf.org/Wall-of-Faces/107/GARY-L-ABRAHAMSON/; interviews with Karen Abrahamson, 31 August, 3 September, 5 September 2012. Interview with Robert Abrahamson, 3 September 2012.
26. Interview with Donita Kay Bliss Abrahamson Brownlee, 10 September 2012.
27. Ibid.; interview with Robert Abrahamson; interview with Karen Abrahamson, 5 September 2012.
28. What follows rests on the detailed history of the 4th of the 506th, David W. Taylor's *Our War: The History and Sacrifices of an Infantry Battalion in the Vietnam War, 1968–1971* (Medina, OH: War Journal Publishing, 2011).
29. Taylor, *Our War*, 15.
30. Ibid., 20.
31. Tim O'Brien, *If I Die in a Combat Zone: Box Me Up and Ship Me Home* (New York: Delacorte, 1973).
32. Taylor, *Our War*, 421–23; Gen. H. Norman Schwarzkopf with Peter Petre, *It Doesn't Take a Hero* (New York: Bantam Books, 1992), 158, 163.
33. Taylor, *Our War*, 441–44; Laughlin quote on 441; 456–58; "no system" quote on 448.
34. Ibid., 467–76, 489–97.
35. Ibid., quote on 498, 499.
36. Interviews with Robert Abrahamson, 3 September 2012, David Abrahamson, 25 September 2012, and Karen Abrahamson, 31 August 2012.
37. David Hackworth and Eilhys England, *Steel My Soldiers' Hearts: The Hopeless to Hardcore Transformation of U.S. Army, 4th Battalion, 39th Infantry, Vietnam* (New York: Rugged Land, LLC, 2002), 303.

38. Ibid., 307–8.
39. Hackworth, "Rest in Peace, Billy Scott," https://www.sun-sentinel.com/2000/04/20/rest-in-peace-billy-scott-you-earned-it/. The Vietnam Veterans Memorial lists him as Robert Eugene Spiegal.
40. Hackworth and England, *Steel My Soldiers' Hearts*, 308–9.
41. Ibid., 311–12.
42. Ibid., 303.
43. Email from Gary Rogers to the author, 17 December 2016.
44. Ibid.
45. https://www.vvmf.org/Wall-of-Faces/38268/WALTER-L-NUTT-III/.
46. Dr. Byron E. Holley, *Vietnam, 1968–1969: A Battalion Surgeon's Journal* (Lincoln, NE: iUniverse.com, 2000), 171.
47. Walter Nutt's DSC citation can be found at https://militaryhallofhonor.com/honoree-record.php?id=268096.

Chapter 8

1. Basil Paquet, "Poems from the Vietnam War," *New York Review of Books*, 18 December 1969. A few months earlier, *Sticks and Bones*, an antiwar play by the veteran David Rabe, opened at Villanova University in 1969. The play opened in New York, along with Rabe's *The Basic Training of Pavlo Hummel*, in 1971. See Rabe, *The Vietnam Plays*, vol. 1 (New York: Grove Press, 1993). Among the earliest memoirs, see Ronald J. Glasser, MD, *365 Days* (New York: George Braziller, 1971). Others include Tim O'Brien, *If I Die in a Combat Zone* (New York: Delacorte Press, 1973); Ron Kovic, *Born on the Fourth of July* (New York: Simon & Shuster, 1976); Philip Caputo, *A Rumor of War* (New York: Holt, Rinehart and Winston, 1977).
2. Paquet, "Poems from the Vietnam War."
3. Ibid.
4. Larry Rottmann, Jan Barry, and Basil T. Paquet, eds., *Winning Hearts and Minds: War Poems by Vietnam Veterans* (Brooklyn, NY: 1st Casualty Press, 1972), 37, 56, 20, 3. On Barry, Rottmann, and VVAW, see Gerald Nicosia, *Home to War: A History of the Vietnam Veterans'*

Movement (New York: Crown Publishing, 2001).

5. Paquet, emails to author, 30 October, 16 November 2023.
6. Stephen Spender, "Poetry of the Unspeakable," *New York Review of Books*, 8 February 1973; W. D. Ehrhart, "Soldier Poets of the Vietnam War," *Virginia Quarterly Review*, Spring 1987; Paquet interview, 20 November 2023.
7. Reviews of W*inning Hearts and Minds* are on the inner flaps of the first edition's dust jacket. Wayne Carlin, Basil T. Paquet, Larry Rottmann, eds., *Free Fire Zone: Short Stories by Vietnam Veterans* (New York: McGraw-Hill, 1973). Paquet, "Is Anyone Guilty? If So, Who?," review of Mary McCarthy's *Medina, New York Review of Books*, 21 September 1972. "Postmortem," along with the records of 1st Casualty Press, are in Archives and Special Collections, University of Connecticut Library. Paquet, phone interview with author, 20 November 2023.
8. Paquet, phone interview with author, 2 November 2023 and email to author 30 October 2023. Basil Bradley Paquet obituary, *Saratogian*, 24 July 2012.
9. Paquet, emails to author, 30 October 2023, 16 November 2023.
10. These were antiwar positions widely held at the time but since challenged by historians of Vietnam; see Peter Zinoman, "Review" of Mark Philip Bradley, *Vietnam at War, H-Diplo Roundtable*, vol. II, no. 7, 2011; Christopher Goscha, *The Road to Dien Bien Phu: A History of the First War for Vietnam* (Princeton: Princeton University Press, 2022), among others.
11. Paquet email to author, 30 October 2013; *United States v. Seeger*, 1965.
12. His claim as the first non-religious CO in Connecticut can be found in "Basil Paquet on His Experience in Vietnam." The talk was first given in 2002 and was posted on the University of Miami, Library Archives, Sixties Collection on 13 August 2021; Paquet, phone interview author, 2 November 2023.
13. "Basil Paquet on His Experience in Vietnam"; Paquet, email to author, 30 October 2023. A contrary view of medical training can

be found in my *"War Stories,"* 7.

14. Paquet, email to author, 30 October 2023.
15. Paquet emails to author, 30 October, 16 November 2023.
16. Ibid.
17. Paquet, email to author, 18 November 2023; Nicosia, *Home to War*, 140–44.
18. Paquet, emails to author; phone interview with author, 20 November 2023.
19. Paquet, emails to author; Sheryl Gifford, "'this is how I know myself': a conversation with Sandra Pouchet Paquet," https://smallaxe.net/sxsalon/interviews/how-i-know-myself; Sandra Paquet cv, https://english.as.miami.edu/_assets/pdf/sandra-paquet-cv.pdf.
20. Paquet, email to author, 16 November 2023; Tim O'Brien, *The Things They Carried* (Boston: Houghton Mifflin, 1990); Michael Herr, *Dispatches* (New York: Alfred A. Knopf, 1977); Karl Marlantes, *Matterhorn: A Novel of the Vietnam War* (New York: Atlantic Monthly Press, 2010); Norman Mailer, *The Naked and the Dead* (New York: Rinehart and Company, 1948). For a critical view of Herr and O'Brien, see my *"War Stories,"* 26–32.
21. "Basil Paquet on His Experience in Vietnam."
22. Ibid.
23. Paquet, email to author, 21 November 2023
24. Ibid.,
25. Ibid. Paquet, email to author, 16 November 2023.
26. Kulik, *"War Stories,"* 257.

Epilogue

1. Philip Caputo, A *Rumor of War* (New York: Henry Holt, 1996); Ron Kovic, *Born on the Fourth of July* (New York: McGraw Hill, 1976); Lynda Van Devanter, *Home Before Morning* (New York: Beaufort Books, 1983); Michael Herr, *Dispatches* (New York: Avon, 1978); Tim O'Brien, *The Things They Carried* (New York: Houghton Mifflin, 1990), 28. For critiques of Caputo and Van Devanter, see my *"War Stories,"* 171–80, 53–68.

2. "Ronald Reagan's Remarks to Veterans of Foreign Wars Convention, (VFW)," Chicago, Illinois, 18 August 1980, YouTube, https://www.youtube.com/watch?v=RbZGghczhs4&t=4s, accessed 18 January 2023.

3. On its own, as opposed to a rejoinder to this book, a study of those who conned their way out of the draft would be enlightening. Begin with James Fallows, "What Did You Do in the Class War, Daddy?", *Washington Monthly*, 1 October 1975; Mark Helprin, "I Dodged the Draft, and I Was Wrong," *Wall Street Journal*, 16 October 1992; John Lithgow, *Drama: An Actor's Education* (New York: HarperCollins, 2011); Peter Schjeldahl, "The Art of Dying," *The New Yorker*, 16 December 2019; and Michael Kazin, "What I Saw at the Revolution That Didn't Happen: Memoirs of a Weatherman," *Dissent*, Fall 2023. Only Kazin expressed no regrets. On Trump's view of veterans, see Maggie Astor, "John Kelly, a Former White House Chief of Staff, Confirms Trump's Disparaging of Veterans," *New York Times*, 3 October 2023.

Selected Bibliography

Bartimus, Tad, et al., eds. *War Torn: Stories of War from the Women Reporters Who Covered Vietnam*. New York: Random House, 2002.

Baskir, Lawrence M., and William A. Strauss. *Chance and Circumstance: The Draft, The War and The Vietnam Generation*. New York: Alfred A. Knopf, 1978.

Berrigan, Daniel. *And the Risen Bread: Selected and New Poems*. New York: Fordham University Press, 1998.

Bonanno, George A. *The End of Trauma: How the New Study of Resilience Is Changing How We Think about PTSD*. New York: Basic Books, 2021.

Brock, Peter. *Pacifism in the United States: From the Colonial Era to the First World War*. Princeton: Princeton University Press, 1968.

Chambers, John Whiteclay, II. *To Raise an Army: The Draft Comes to Modern America*. New York: The Free Press, 1987.

Clamurro, William H. *Private Archaeology*. Norman, OK: Quail Creek Editions, 2008.

———. *The Vietnam Typescript*. Emporia, KS: Bluestem Press, 2018.

Coffin, Lesley L. *Lew Ayres: Hollywood's Conscientious Objector*. Jackson: University Press of Mississippi, 2012.

Courtright, David. *Soldiers in Revolt: GI Resistance During the Vietnam War*, 2nd ed. Chicago: Haymarket Books, 2005.

Davis, Roger G. "Conscientious Cooperators: The Seventh-day Adventists and Military Service, 1860–1945." PhD diss., George Washington University, 1970.

Day, Dorothy. *The Long Loneliness: The Autobiography of the Legendary Catholic Social Activist*. New York: Harper & Row, 1952.

DeBenedetti, Charles. *An American Ordeal: The Antiwar Movement of the*

Vietnam Era. Syracuse, NY: Syracuse University Press, 1990.

Dingman, C. Michael. *Unlikely Warrior: Memoirs of a Vietnam Combat Medic*. Maitland, FL: Xulon Press, 2014.

Donahey, Ron. *Vietnam Combat Medic: A Conscientious Objector in the Central Highlands*. Atlanta: Deeds Publishing, 2018.

Eisman, Eugene. *Bitter Medicine: A Doctor's Year in Vietnam*. Privately published, n.d.

Finnegan, James O. *In the Company of Marines: A Surgeon Remembers Vietnam*. Privately published, 2009.

Flynn, George Q. *The Draft: 1940–1973*. Lawrence: University Press of Kansas, 1993.

Ford, Herbert. *No Guns on Their Shoulders*. Nashville, TN: Southern Publishing Association, 1968.

Gioglio, Gerald R., ed. *Days of Decision: An Oral History of Conscientious Objectors in the Military during the Vietnam War*. Trenton, NJ: Broken Rifle Press, 1989.

Goscha, Christopher. *The Road to Dien Bien Phu: A History of the First War for Vietnam*. Princeton: Princeton University Press, 2022.

Hackworth, Col. David H., and Eilhys England. *Steel My Soldiers' Hearts: The Hopeless to Hardcore Transformation of U.S. Army, 4th Battalion, 39th Infantry, Vietnam*. New York: Rugged Land, 2002.

Hagan, John. *Northern Passage: American Vietnam War Resisters in Canada*. Cambridge, MA: Harvard University Press, 2001.

Herman, Jan K., ed. *Navy Medicine in Vietnam: Oral Histories from Dien Bien Phu to the Fall of Saigon*. Jefferson, NC: McFarland and Company, 2009.

Hochschild, Adam. *American Midnight: The Great War, a Violent Peace, and Democracy's Forgotten Crisis*. New York: Mariner Books, 2022.

Karlin, Wayne, Basil T. Paquet, and Larry Rottmannn, eds. *Free Fire Zone: Short Stories by Vietnam Veterans*. New York: McGraw-Hill, 1973.

Kearney, James C., and William H. Clamurro. *Duty to Serve, Duty to Conscience: The Story of Two Conscientious Objector Medics during the Vietnam War*. Denton: University of North Texas Press, 2023.

Kellogg, Walter Guest. *The Conscientious Objector*. New York: Boni and

Liveright, 1919.

Kelly, Tobias. *Battles of Conscience: British Pacifists and the Second World War*. London: Chatto and Windus, 2022.

Kohn, Stephen M. *Jailed for Peace: The History of American Draft Law Violators, 1658–1985*. New York: Praeger, 1986.

Krehbiel, Nicholas A. *General Louis B. Hershey and Conscientious Objection During World War II*. Columbia: University of Missouri Press, 2011.

Kulik, Gary. *"War Stories": False Atrocity Tales, Swift Boaters, and Winter Soldiers—What Really Happened in Vietnam*. Washington, DC: Potomac Books, 2009.

Lee, David. *Sergeant York: An American Hero*. Lexington: University Press of Kentucky, 1988.

Lynd, Alice, ed. *We Won't Go: Personal Accounts of War Objectors*. Boston, MA: Beacon Press, 1968.

Lynd, Alice, and Staughton Lynd. *Stepping Stones: Memoir of a Life Together*. New York: Lexington Books, 2009.

Mansavage, Jean Anne. "'A Sincere and Meaningful Belief': Legal Conscientious Objection During the Vietnam War." PhD diss., Texas A&M University, 2000.

Maraniss, David. *They Marched into Sunlight: War and Peace, Vietnam and America, October, 1967*. New York: Simon & Schuster, 2003.

McKeown, Bonni. *Peaceful Patriot: The Story of Tom Bennett*. Capon Springs, WV: Peaceful Patriot Press, 1980.

McNally, Richard J. *Remembering Trauma*. Cambridge: Harvard University Press, 2003.

Merton, Thomas. *Raids on the Unspeakable*. New York: New Directions, 1964.

Mills, Randy K. *Troubled Hero: A Medal of Honor, Vietnam and the War at Home*. Bloomington: Indiana University Press, 2006.

Morris, David J. *The Evil Hours: A Biography of Post-Traumatic Stress Disorder*. New York: Houghton-Mifflin-Harcourt, 2015.

Moskos, Charles C., and John Whiteclay Chambers II, eds. *The New Conscientious Objection: From Sacred to Secular Resistance*. New York: Oxford University Press, 1993.

SELECTED BIBLIOGRAPHY

Nelson, Jacquelyn S. *Indiana Quakers Confront the Civil War*. Bloomington: Indiana Historical Society, 1991.

Nicosia, Gerald. *Home to War: A History of the Vietnam Veterans' Movement*. New York: Crown Publishers, 2001.

Nolen, Keith. *Ripcord: Screaming Eagles Under Siege*. Novato, CA: Presidio Press, 2000.

O'Brien, Tim. *If I Die in a Combat Zone: Box Me Up and Ship Me Home*. New York: Dell Publishing, 1973.

———. *The Things They Carried*. Boston, MA: Houghton Mifflin, 1990.

Phelan, Andrew L. *"Free": Letters and Remembrances of Vietnam with a Selection of Civil War Letters Written by Eugene Kingman*. Norman, OK: Quail Creek Publishing, 2006.

Prados, John, and Ray W. Stubbe. *Valley of Decision: The Siege of Khe Sanh*. New York: Houghton Mifflin, 1991.

Pringle, Cyrus. *The Record of a Quaker Conscience, Cyrus Pringle's Diary*. Middletown, DE: n.p., reprint 2020.

Riley, Sabrina. "Medical Cadet Corps." 29 January 2020, encyclopedia.adventist.org.

Rios, Abel. "Vietnam War and Seventh-Day Adventists." 10 May 2022, encyclopedia.adventist.org.

Robbins, Mary Susannah, ed. *Against the Vietnam War: Writings by Activists*. Rev. ed. New York: Rowman and Littlefield, 1999.

Roberson, Cliff. *Vietnam Medic: Field Journal*. Ukiah, CA: CaeSaR Books, 2011.

Rottmann, Larry, et al., eds. *Winning Hearts and Minds: War Poems by Vietnam Veterans*. New York: McGraw-Hill, 1972.

Rutenberg, Amy J. *Rough Draft: Cold War Military Manpower Policy and the Origins of Vietnam-Era Draft Resistance*. Ithaca: Cornell University Press, 2019.

Sallah, Michael, and Mitch Weiss. *Tiger Force: A True Story of Men and War*. New York: Little, Brown and Company, 2006.

Schlissel, Lillian, ed. *Conscience in America: A Documentary History of Conscientious Objection in America, 1757–1967*. New York: E. P. Dutton & Co., 1968.

Sibley, Mulford Q., and Philip E. Jacob. *Conscription of Conscience: The American State and the Conscientious Objector, 1940–1947*. Ithaca: Cornell University Press, 1952.

Skeyhill, Tom, ed. *Sergeant York: His Own Life Story and War Diary*. New York: Racehorse Publishing, 2018.

Spalding, Arthur W. *Origin and History of Seventh-Day Adventists*, 4 vols. Washington, DC: Review and Herald Publishing, 1961.

Stahl, John, ed. *Hutterite CO's in World War I: Stories, Diaries, and Other Accounts from the United States Military Camps*. Hawley, MN: Spring Prairie Publishing, 1997.

Stoltzfus, Duane C. S. *Pacifists in Chains: The Persecution of Hutterites during the Great War*. Baltimore: Johns Hopkins University Press, 2013.

Stubbe, Chaplain Ray William. *Battalion of Kings: A Tribute to Our Fallen Brothers Who Died Because of the Battlefield of Khe Sanh, Vietnam*. 2nd ed., revised. Wauwatosa, WI: Khe Sanh Veterans, Inc., 2005.

Taylor, David W. *Our War: The History and Sacrifices of an Infantry Battalion in the Vietnam War, 1968–1971*. Medina, OH: War Journal Publishing, 2011.

Thomas, Louisa. *Conscience: Two Soldiers, Two Pacifists, One Family—A Test of Will and Faith in World War I*. New York: Penguin Press, 2011.

Thomas, Norman. *The Conscientious Objector*. New York: B. W. Huebsch, 1923.

Tollefson, James W. *The Strength Not to Fight: Conscientious Objectors of the Vietnam War*. Washington, DC: Brassey's, 2000.

Valentine, Gilbert M. *J. N. Andrews: Mission Pioneer, Evangelist, and Thought Leader*. Nampa, ID: Pacific Press, 2019.

Wells, Tom. *The War Within: America's Battle Over Vietnam*. Berkeley: University of California Press, 1994.

Wiest, Andrew. *The Boys of '67: Charlie Company's War in Vietnam*. New York: Osprey Publishing, 2012.

———. *Charlie Company's Journey Home: The Boys of '67 and the War They Left Behind*. New York: Osprey Publishing, 2018.

Wilcox, Francis McLellan. *Seventh-day Adventists in Time of War*. Washington, DC: Review and Herald Publishing, 1936.

Ybarra, Lea, ed. *Vietnam Veteranos: Chicanos Recall the War*. Austin: University of Texas Press, 2004.

Young, Allan. *The Harmony of Illusions: Inventing Post-Traumatic Stress Disorder*. Princeton: Princeton University Press, 1998.

Zaroulis, Nancy, and Gerald Sullivan. *Who Spoke Up? American Protest Against the War in Vietnam, 1963–1975*. New York: Doubleday, 1984.

Index

A Shau Valley, 42–43
Abrahamson, David, 110
Abrahamson, Donita, 106–7, 110
Abrahamson, Gary Lee
    background, 10, 106–7
    basic and medical training, 106
    decision to serve, 106
    military service in Vietnam, 107, 109–10
    Vietnam War casualty, 10, 106, 110
Abrahamson, Karen, 107, 110
Abrahamson, Robert, 106, 107
absolutists, 21–22
Abzug, Bella, 51
Adventists. *See* Seventh-day Adventists
Afghanistan war, 32
Agnew, Spiro, 120
Akhmatova, Anna, 39
All Quiet on the Western Front (film), 26–27
Alpha Company, 66–67
"altruistic suicide," 76–79
Amana communitarians, 17
American Legion, 25
American Revolution, 14
An Khê Pass, 75–76
Anabaptists, 14–15. *See also* Hutterites
Anderson, George, 70, 80
Anderson, James, Jr., 75
Annamite Mountains, 109–10
antibiotic trials. *See* Operation Whitecoat
Apocalypse Now (film), 125
Army Medical Corps. *See* Operation Whitecoat

Ashworth, Shelton, 109
Ayres, Lew, 26–27

Bahá'í faith, x, 10, 31
Baker, Newton, 19–20, 21
Baltimore Friends, 15
Band of Brothers ethos, 77–78
Banda, George, 66–67
Baptists, 10, 31
Barry, Jan, 116, 120
Benn, Laura, 59
Bennett, Thomas W., 10
Berrigan, Daniel, 5, 49
Berrigan brothers, 49
Bill of Rights, 14
Bình Định Province, 8–9, 91
Bliss, Donita, 106–7, 110
Blue (Mitchell), 35
Born on the Fourth of July (Kovic), 125
The Boston Globe, 51–52, 53
Boykins, Rudy, 91–92, 93
Bradley, William, 66–67
Brathwaite, Roger Clayton, 10
Brethren, x, 3, 7, 24
Buddhism, x, 33, 99, 103
Burns, Ken, 125–26
Butler, Joe, 60
Byrd, Byron, 58
Byrd, Nolan
    background, 57–58
    basic and medical training, 59–60
    military service in Vietnam, 60
    Vietnam War casualty, 60–61

INDEX

Cambodia, 8, 63, 93
Camp Detrick, 29–30
Camp Funston, 19–20
Camp Gordon, 21
Canada, 23, 99
Cannon, Joe, 111
Caputo, Philip, 84, 115, 117, 125
Carnegie, Andrew, 18
Castillo, "Doc," 109
Catholics. *See* Roman Catholics
Chambers, John Whiteclay, 31
Chicago Sun-Times, 117
Christadelphians, 18
Christy, Michael, 63–65
Chu Lai, 107, 108–9
Church of God, 18
Civilian Public Service (CPS) program, 25, 27
Civil War, 3, 14–17, 18
claims of conscience, 14–16
Clark, Earl K., 70
Clemons, Joseph, 108–9
closure, 36, 77, 123–24
Coffin, William Sloane, 120
Cohen, Margie, 50
Cole, Gordon Eugene
　background, 104
　basic training, 104–5
　decision to serve, 104
　medical training, 105
　military service in Vietnam, 105
　Vietnam casualty, 105–6
Cole, Sandy, 103–6
Coming Home (film), 125
Commandments, x, 3, 17
communitarians, 17
Concepcion-Nieves, David, 109
Confucianism, 33
conscience, claims of, 14–16
conscientious cooperators, 26, 57. *See also* Seventh-day Adventists
conscientious objection
　defined, ix, 3, 31, 33
　post-enlistment claim of, 69, 70–72, 75
conscientious objector (CO) medics in Vietnam
　deaths of, 10, 49, 60–61, 67, 73, 105–6, 109–13
　grey zone occupied by, x, 4–5, 11, 126–27
　honoring, 125–26, 127
　journalism career following, 47, 49, 51–56
　memoirs by, 81–96 (*See also* Dingman, C. Michael; Donahey, Ron; Roberson, Cliff)
　overview of medics' stories, ix, 7–10, 28–29, 32, 126–27
　pantheist from California, 33–46
　poetry and fiction written by, 39, 100, 115–17, 121, 123 (*See also* Paquet, Basil T.)
　Roman Catholics, 7, 9, 47–56, 119
　Seventh-day Adventists, 7, 8, 9, 10, 28–31, 57–67, 81–96, 104–10 (*See also* Operation Whitecoat)
　statistics, 3, 4, 28, 31–32, 57
　stories of courage, 97–113 (*See also* Abrahamson, Gary Lee; Cole, Gordon Eugene; Kays, Kenneth M.)
Corps of Engineers, 20, 25
Cox, Orville, 26
CPS (Civilian Public Service) program, 25, 27
Crayton, Melvin, 53
Crosby, Gene, 30
Crosby, Rhonda, 30
Củ Chi, 51

Đà Nẵng, 84
Dahl, Larry G., 75–76
The Daily Illini, 102
Day, Dorothy, 5, 49
The Deer Hunter (film), 125

Devanter, Lynda Van, 125
Diller, Jay Thomas
    background, 57, 59, 61, 65
    basic and medical training, 65
    military service in Vietnam, 65–66
    Vietnam War casualty, 66
Dills, Ronald Eugene, 109
Dingman, Barbara, 95
Dingman, C. Michael
    background, 81
    basic training, 83
    decision to serve, 82, 83
    military service in Vietnam, 85–87, 91–93
    post-Vietnam life, 95–96
    willingness to bear arms, 85–86, 92
Dispatches (Herr), 78, 121–22
Đổi Mới (renovation), 55
Donahey, Dorothy, 84, 88–89
Donahey, Ron
    background, 81
    basic and medical training, 82–83, 84
    decision to serve, 82
    military service in Vietnam, 84, 85–89
    post-Vietnam life, 93–94, 96
    willingness to bear arms, 85–88, 89
Doss, Desmond, 26, 82
Dragon Valley, 109–10
Durkheim, Émile, 76–77
"dying in vain" question, 77–78

Eastern Orthodox Church, 31
Eastern religions, x, 33, 99, 102–3
Egan, Greg, 62
Ehrhart, Bill, 125
Episcopalians, x, 3, 10, 31
The Evil Hours (Morris), 34

Federal Enrollment Act (1863), 14–15
Feldman, Ed, 80
Ferlinghetti, Lawrence, 39
Ferruzzi, Ron, 125
5th Battalion of the 46th Infantry, 107–10
Finnigan, James, 72–73, 74
Firak, Anthony Marian, 53
1st Casualty Press, 116, 117, 120, 121
Ford, Henry, 18
Fort Detrick, 29–30
Fort Sam Houston, 6–7, 28, 39, 59–60, 104–5, 112
France, 23
Free Fire Zone (short story collection), 117
Friends. *See* Quakers
Fry, James, 17
FSB Henderson, 66–67
Fujii, Dennis M., 78
Fussell, Paul, 79–80
Fuzzy (soldier), 35, 36, 44, 45

Galloway, Joseph L., 84
Gandhian, x
Garcia, Benjamin, 91
Garrison, William Lloyd, 17
Garski, Ken, 62
German religious sects, 14, 18
Gerstal, Howard, 90, 95
Gilmore, William Allen, 88–89
Girouard, James, 28
Great Britain, 22–23
Green, Richard Hershel "Richie," 50, 53, 56
Gross, E., 112
"Group Shot" (unpublished poetry collection), 123

Hackworth, David, 44, 110, 111, 112
Haeusserman, Michael, 92
Hall, John, 60
Hall, William
    background, 57, 59–60
    basic training, 59–60
    military service in Vietnam, 60
    post-Vietnam life, 60–61, 67
    on Whitecoat program, 60

Hartford Courant, 117
Hawley, Richard A., 66
Haynes, Carlyle B., 26
Hemingway, Ernest, 79
"heroic suicide," 76–79
Herr, Michael, 78, 121–22, 125
Hersh, Seymour, 29
Hershey, Lewis B., 24–25, 27
Hinduism, 99, 103
Hirst, Tom
    background, 57–58, 59, 60, 61
    basic and medical training, 61–62
    decision to serve, 57
    military service in Vietnam, 62–65
    on Operation Whitecoat, 31, 61–62
    post-Vietnam life, 67
    willingness to bear arms, 8, 62
Hồ Chí Minh, 5, 55, 118
Ho Chi Minh Trail, 126
Hofer, Joseph, 22
Hofer, Michael, 22
Holley, Byron, 113
Home Before Morning (Van Devanter), 125
House Appropriations Committee, 52
Hubenthal, John
    background, 33, 37–38
    basic and medical training, 34, 39–41
    decision to serve, 36, 38–39, 46
    military service in Vietnam, 33, 34–35, 41–45
    poetry by, 39
    post-Vietnam life, 33–34, 35–37, 45–46
    on Whitecoat program, 40
    willingness to bear arms, 43
Hubenthal, Wendy, 34
Hudson, Rick, 111
Hutterites, 18, 19, 20, 21–22

If I Die in a Combat Zone (O'Brien), 80, 108
Indiana Friends, 16

Inest Clementia Forti (motto), 78
Iraq war, 32, 56
Israelitish House of David, 18

Jarrell, Randall, 118
Jehovah's Witnesses, 18, 24
Jews, 9–10
Johnson, Bruce, 65
Johnson, Gerald, 53
Johnson, Lyndon, 48, 107–8
Johnson, Tom, 64

Karlin, Wayne, 117, 121
Kays, John and Ethel, 98
Kays, Kenneth M.
    background, 98–99
    decision to serve, 98, 99–100
    military service in Vietnam, 97–98, 100
    poetry by, 100
    post-Vietnam life, 100–103
    willingness to bear arms, 97, 98
Kazickas, Jurate, 73–74, 77
Kennedy, David M., 19, 21
Kerry, John, 51, 52, 120–21
Khan, Khizr, 56
Khe Sanh siege (1968), 69–75, 80. *See also* Spicer, Jonathan
Kiến Phong Province, 112, 113
"kindly considerations," 20–21
Kinman, Duane, 26
Kohn, Stephen M., 31
Kon Tum Province, 88
Korean War, 27–28
Kosky, Mike, 87
Kovic, Ron, 115, 117, 125
Kulik, Gary
    background, 5–6
    on *Band of Brothers* ethos, 77–78
    basic and medical training, 6–8, 33, 41, 83, 86
    on closure, 124
    on "conscientious objector" term, 3

INDEX

decision to serve, ix, 4–6, 10, 11, 49, 56, 118–19, 126
military service in Vietnam, 8–9, 87, 95, 119
post-Vietnam life, 125
on PTSD, 36
willingness to bear arms, 8, 86

Laughlin, Mike, 109
Lê Duẩn, 55
Leaderbrand, Preston, 88
Leaves of Grass (Whitman), 38
Lincoln, Abraham, 16
Long Barracks, 6–7, 28, 31, 59–60
Long Binh, 119–20
Long Son, 109
"long-term" PTSD, 36
The Los Angeles Times, 73
Lutherans, 3, 31, 72

Madison, James, 14
Magilligan, Don, 73
Mailer, Norman, 122
Maraniss, David, 52
Marlantes, Karl, 122, 125–26
Marlin, Ellis Sanford, 50, 53
Martinez, Ruben D., 84, 89
Matterhorn (Marlantes), 122
McCain, John, 55
McCarley, Kenneth W., 108
McCarthy, Mary, 117
McCormack, John, 4
McGraw Hill, 117, 121
McNally, Richard J., 36–37
Medical Cadet Corps (MCC), 9, 26, 82
medics. *See* conscientious objector medics in Vietnam
Medina (McCarthy), 117
Mekong Delta, 112
Mennonites
  American Revolution military service by, 16
  background, x, 3, 14

World War I military service by, 18, 19, 20
World War II military service by, 24
Merton, Thomas, 5
Methodists, x, 3, 31
Military Conscientious Objector Act (1992), 32
Miller, Jeff, 91
Miller, William, 17
Missouri Synod Lutherans, 31
Mitchell, Joni, 35
Molokans, 18, 21
Montagnards, 85
Moore, Harold G., 84
Moravians, 14
Moreno, Michael, 10
Morris, David, 34
Musgrave, John, 125
Mỹ Đồng, 106
My Lai, 107, 108, 117

The Naked and the Dead (Mailer), 122
The New York Review of Books, 115, 116, 117, 120
The New York Times, 47–48, 117
Newsweek, 117
Nixon, Richard, 29, 48, 77, 101, 126
noncombatant military service
  in American colonies, 13–14
  Civil War, 3, 14–17, 18
  Korean War, 27–28
  overview, 3–4, 13, 32, 57
  post-Vietnam War, 32
  Vietnam War, 4, 27–32 (*See also* conscientious objector medics in Vietnam)
  World War I, 18–23, 25, 79
  World War II, 3–4, 23–27, 31–32, 82
non-resistance. *See* pacifism
Novick, Lynn, 125–26
Nutt, Wally "Tiny"
  background, 112, 113
  basic training, 112

167

INDEX

military service in Vietnam,
    111, 112–13
Vietnam War casualty, 111–12, 113
willingness to bear arms, 112, 113

O'Brien, Tim, 78–80, 108, 115, 121, 125
Ohlson, Carl, 111
Olson, Charles, 120
O'Neill, Tip, 52
Operation Desert Storm, 32
Operation Lam Son 719, 78
Operation Whitecoat
    Abrahamson (Robert) and, 106
    background, 9, 28, 29–31, 61–62
    Dingman and, 83
    Hall and, 60
    Hirst and, 61, 62
    Hubenthal and, 40
    Rogers and, 112
Owen, Wilfred, 79, 118

pacifism, 3, 5, 13–17, 18–19
Paine, Thomas, 38
Pantheists, 9, 33. *See also* Hubenthal, John
Pape, Joseph, 117
Paquet, Basil T.
    background, 117–19
    basic and medical training, 115, 119
    on closure, 123–124
    decision to serve, 118–19
    military service in Vietnam, 115–16, 119–20, 121, 122–23
    poetry and fiction by, 115–17, 121, 123
    post-Vietnam life, 115–17, 120–24
Paquet, Sandra Pouchet, 121
Pershing, (general), 23
Perth Amboy Evening News, 51
Philadelphia Sunday Bulletin, 117
Phu Bai, 85
Phú Thọ Province, 43
Pleiku, 10, 84, 85

"Poems from the Vietnam War," in *The New York Review of Books*, 115
Poese, Nigel Frederick, 111
poetry and fiction by conscientious objectors, 39, 100, 115–17, 121, 123
Politico, 52
"Postmortem" (unpublished poetry and fiction collection), 117, 121
Pouchet, Sandra, 121
Pringle, Cyrus, 15–16
Protestantism, 7, 13
PTSD
    description of, 34
    Dingman's experience, 95–96
    Donahey's experience, 93, 96
    Hall's experience, 67
    Hubenthal's experience, 35–36
    "long-term" PTSD, 36
    Roberson's experience, 94–95, 96
    study of, 36–37

Quakers
    background, x, 13–14
    on Civil War military service, 15–16
    Vietnam War military service by, 111
    World War I military service by, 21
    World War II military service by, 24, 25
Quan River, 109–10
Quang, Nguyen Kim, 54
Quảng Ngãi City, 108–9
Quartermaster Corps, 20, 25
Quy Nhơn, 84

Randolph, John, 73, 74
Reagan, Ronald, 125
Reimer, Jeffrey W., 77
resilience, 37, 96
"Re-Up Hill," 66
Ribera, Tony, 90, 95
Roberson, Cliff
    background, 81
    decision to serve, 82, 83–84

military service in Vietnam, 84–87, 89–91
post-Vietnam life, 94–95, 96
willingness to bear arms, 85–86, 91
Roberson, Jenny, 94
Rogerenes, 17
Rogers, David
  background, 48–49
  basic training, 49
  decision to serve, 47, 48–49, 51, 55, 56, 122, 127
  military service in Vietnam, 47, 49–51
  post-Vietnam life, 47, 49, 51–56
  on Trump's draft deferment, 55–56
  willingness to bear arms, 50
Rogers, Gary W., 112
Rogers, Rebecca, 51
Roman Catholics
  background, x, 3
  Vietnam War military service by, 7, 9, 47–56, 119
  World War II military service by, 31
Roosevelt, Franklin, 24
Roosevelt, Theodore, 19, 20
Rottmann, Larry, 116, 117, 120, 121
A Rumor of War (Caputo), 84, 125
Russell, Wayne, 49, 53
Russellites, 18
Russian Molokans, 18, 21

St. Louis Post-Dispatch, 117
Saints of Christ, 18
Sandburg, Carl, 39
San Nicholas, Victor "Guam," 91–92
Sassoon, Siegfried, 79, 118
Sayre, John Nevin, 20
Schrang (sergeant), 92
Schrenk, Don, 90, 95
Schwartzkopf, Norman H., 108
Schweitzer, Albert, 70
Scott, Billy, 110–11
Scruggs, Jan, 53
Scully, James, 120

SDA. *See* Seventh-day Adventists
Second Amendment, 14
Seeger, United States v. (1965), x, 31, 33, 119
Selective Service Act (1917), 18, 20–21, 22, 23–24
Selective Service Act (1948), 27
Selective Training and Service Act (1940), 23–24
selfless actions (self-sacrifice), 75–80, 125
Seventh-day Adventists (SDA)
  background, x, 7, 17, 18, 57, 61
  Civil War military service by, 17
  Korean War military service by, 28
  Vietnam War military service by, 7, 8, 9, 10, 28–31, 57–67, 81–96, 104–10, 126. (*See also* Operation Whitecoat)
  World War I military service by, 20, 23
  World War II military service by, 26, 82
Sewell, Karen, 67
Sewell, Terry
  background, 57, 58–59, 61
  post-Vietnam life, 67
Shade, Dave, 10
Shakers, 17
Signal Corps, 25
Sixth Commandment, x, 17
Slaughterhouse-Five (Vonnegut), 35
Sluiter, Larry, 104, 106
Smitty (soldier), 91
Society of Friends, 13. *See also* Quakers
Sông Bé, 62
Spender, Stephen, 117, 120
Spicer, Jonathan
  background, 69
  basic training, 70
  decision to serve, 69, 70
  military service in Vietnam, 69–75, 78, 80
  post-enlistment conscientious objection by, 69, 70–72, 75

Vietnam War casualty, 73
willingness to bear arms, 70, 75, 80
Spiegle, Eugene R., 111
Spillers, George, 91
Stansberry, Larry, 64
Stanton, William, 15, 16
Steiner, David, 99
Sterba, James, 47–48, 52
Stierheim, Richard L., 23
Stimson, Henry, 25–26
stretcher-bearer, 69–80. *See also* Spicer, Jonathan
Stubbe, Ray, 69–72, 77, 80
suicide, 76–79, 102–3
Sullivan, Dan, 72, 80
survivor's guilt, 102, 103

Taoism, 33
The Things They Carried (O'Brien), 78–80, 121
Thomas, Dylan, 116, 118
Thomas, Evan, 22
Thomas, Norman, 22
Thon, Tom, 64
Thoreau, Henry David, 38
Thừa Thiên Province, 43, 97
Tiger Force: A True Story of Men and War, 44
Tiger Mountain, 93
Toledo Blade, 44
Townsend (colonel), 16
Townsend, Joseph, 14
Truman, Harry, 26, 27
Trump, Donald, 55–56, 126
Tschetter, Peter, 20
Tufts, Henry, 44
Turner, Robert, 66–67
24th Evacuation Hospital, 119–20
Tyler, Willie, 89, 91, 95

United States v. Seeger (1965), x, 31, 33, 119

vaccine trials, 28, 29–31. *See also* Whitecoat program
Vietnam, 1968–1969: A Battalion Surgeon's Journal (Byron), 113
Vietnam Veterans Against the War (VVAW), 116, 120–21
Vietnam Veterans Memorial, 53, 125
Vietnam War
conscientious objector medics' stories, ix, 7–10, 28–29, 32, 126–27 (*See also* conscientious objector medics in Vietnam)
disillusionment memoirs and films, 125
"dying in vain" question, 77–78
honoring for veterans, 125–26, 127
poetry and fiction by conscientious objectors, 39, 100, 115–17, 121, 123
The Vietnam War (film), 125–26
Vonnegut, Kurt, 35
VVAW (Vietnam Veterans Against the War), 116, 120–21

Waldner, Joseph, 20
The Wall Street Journal, 48, 52, 53–55
"War Stories" (Kulik), 83
war trauma, study of, 36–37
Wayne County Press, 99
Welsh v. United States (1970), 31
Wenger, Ray, 67
We Were Soldiers Once (Moore and Galloway), 84
White, Ellen Gould, 7, 17
White, James, 17
Whitecoat program. *See* Operation Whitecoat
Whitman, Walt, 38, 39
Williams, Robert "Pud," 98, 101
Wilson, Woodrow, 18, 19, 20, 22, 24
Winning Hearts and Minds: War Poems by Vietnam Veterans (anthology), 116, 117

Woods, Leonard, 19
Woodstock (music festival), 99
World War I, 18–23, 25, 79
World War II, 3–4, 5, 23–27, 29, 31–32, 82
Wright (sergeant), 106
Wright, Mickey, 64

Ybarra, Sam, 44–45
Yeats, William Butler, 118
Yevtushenko, Yevgeny, 39
York, Alvin, 21
Young, Allan, 36

About the Author

Gary Kulik served as a deputy director of the Winterthur Museum, Garden & Library, near Wilmington, Delaware. Previously, he was a department head and assistant director of the Smithsonian's National Museum of American History and the editor of *American Quarterly*. A graduate of St. Michael's College, he earned a PhD in American Civilization at Brown University. He has written extensively on early American industrial history. He is also a decorated veteran of the Vietnam War, having served as a medic in the 4th Infantry Division and as an adjutant's clerk in the 61st Medical Battalion. He is the author of *"War Stories": False Atrocity Tales, Swift Boaters, and Winter Soldiers—What Really Happened in Vietnam* (2009). He lives in Wilmington, Delaware.

Author photo by David Heitur